P9-CAO-580

UNITED STATES HISTORY

CIVIL WAR TO THE PRESENT

Guided Reading Workbook

ISBN   978-0-544-66903-1

4 5 6 7 8 9 10   2536   25 24 23 22 21 20 19

4500767623   C D E F G

Contents

HOW TO USE THIS BOOK

The *Guided Reading Workbook* was developed to help you master United States history content and build your reading and vocabulary skills. Review the next few pages to become familiar with the workbook's features and organization.

Lesson summary pages allow you to interact with the content and key terms and people from each lesson in a module. The summaries explain each lesson of your textbook in a way that is easy to understand.

The Main Ideas statements help focus your attention as you read the summaries.

Definitions for the lesson's Key Terms and People are listed before the Lesson Summary.

To help you find the content you need, headings in the Lesson Summary match those in your United States History book.

Lesson numbers make it easy to find your place in the workbook.

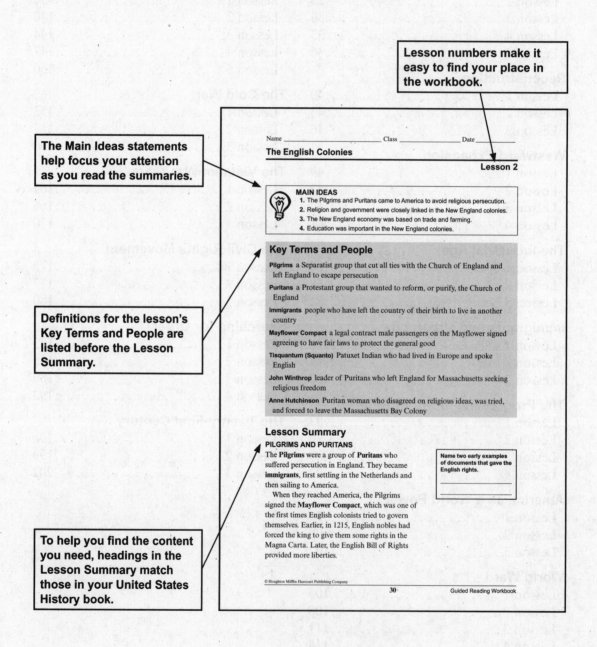

Name _____ Class _____ Date _____

The English Colonies

Lesson 2

MAIN IDEAS
1. The Pilgrims and Puritans came to America to avoid religious persecution.
2. Religion and government were closely linked in the New England colonies.
3. The New England economy was based on trade and farming.
4. Education was important in the New England colonies.

Key Terms and People

Pilgrims a Separatist group that cut all ties with the Church of England and left England to escape persecution

Puritans a Protestant group that wanted to reform, or purify, the Church of England

immigrants people who have left the country of their birth to live in another country

Mayflower Compact a legal contract male passengers on the Mayflower signed agreeing to have fair laws to protect the general good

Tisquantum (Squanto) Patuxet Indian who had lived in Europe and spoke English

John Winthrop leader of Puritans who left England for Massachusetts seeking religious freedom

Anne Hutchinson Puritan woman who disagreed on religious ideas, was tried, and forced to leave the Massachusetts Bay Colony

Lesson Summary
PILGRIMS AND PURITANS

The **Pilgrims** were a group of **Puritans** who suffered persecution in England. They became **immigrants**, first settling in the Netherlands and then sailing to America.

When they reached America, the Pilgrims signed the **Mayflower Compact**, which was one of the first times English colonists tried to govern themselves. Earlier, in 1215, English nobles had forced the king to give them some rights in the Magna Carta. Later, the English Bill of Rights provided more liberties.

Name two early examples of documents that gave the English rights.

_____

© Houghton Mifflin Harcourt Publishing Company

30

Guided Reading Workbook

The lesson's Key Terms and People are in bold type to help you find them.

Name _____ Class _____ Date _____

Lesson 2, *continued*

The Pilgrims learned to fertilize their soil from **Tisquantum**. They invited him and 90 Wampanoag guests to a feast now known as Thanksgiving.

Religion and education played important parts in the Pilgrims' lives, which centered on families. Everyone worked hard, and women had rights that they did not have in England.

Puritans and merchants founded the Massachusetts Bay Colony. Tens of thousands of English men, women, and children would immigrate to it. **John Winthrop** led one group. Puritans believed they had a sacred agreement with God to build a Christian colony.

> What was the Puritans' sacred agreement with God?
> _____
> _____

RELIGION AND GOVERNMENT IN NEW ENGLAND

Politics and religion were closely linked in Puritan New England. While some self-government existed, only chosen male church members could vote.

Some Puritans had different religious views from others. Minister Roger Williams supported the separation of the church from politics, so he was made to leave the colony. He founded Providence. **Anne Hutchinson** was also forced to leave the colony because of her ideas that differed from the group.

> Underline the sentence that means women could not vote in Puritan New England.

NEW ENGLAND ECONOMY

The New England colonies had a hard climate and rocky soil, so the kind of farming done in Virginia was impossible there. Instead, they traded goods, fished, built ships, and became skilled craftspeople.

> Compare sources of income in Virginia and New England.
> _____
> _____

EDUCATION IN THE COLONIES

New England parents wanted their children to read the Bible. They made laws requiring the education of children and set up town schools.

© Houghton Mifflin Harcourt Publishing Company

31   Guided Reading Workbook

As you read each summary, be sure to complete the questions and activities in the margin boxes. They help you check your reading comprehension and track important content.

Each lesson has at least one vocabulary activity that will help you to demonstrate your understanding of the Key Terms and People introduced in the lesson.

The Challenge Activity provides an opportunity for you to apply important critical thinking skills to information from the Lesson Summary.

Some vocabulary activities have a word bank. You can use it to help find answers or complete writing activities.

Various activities help you check your knowledge of Key terms and People.

Writing activities require you to include Key Terms and People. Remember to check to make sure that you are using the terms and names correctly.

Name _____ Class _____ Date _____

Lesson 2, *continued*

The colonists also founded Harvard College to teach ministers.

CHALLENGE ACTIVITY

Critical Thinking: Develop Develop three questions about the Pilgrims' contributions and research to answer them.

Anne Hutchinson	Mayflower Compact	Puritans
immigrants	Pilgrims	Tisquantum
John Winthrop		

DIRECTIONS Answer each question by writing a sentence that contains at least one word from the word bank.

1. Who was put on trial for his or her religious ideas and eventually forced out of the colony?

   _____

2. Who are people that leave their country of birth to live in another country?

   _____

3. Who showed the Pilgrims how to fertilize the soil on their farms and helped them establish relations with the chief of the local Wampanoag Indians?

   _____

4. Who led a group of Puritan colonists who left England for Massachusetts in search of religious freedom?

   _____

DIRECTIONS Choose at least five of the terms or names from the word bank. Use these words to write a letter that relates to the lesson.

32   Guided Reading Workbook

U.S. History to 1860

Lesson 1

MAIN IDEAS
1. Christopher Columbus sailed across the Atlantic Ocean and reached a continent with cultures previously unknown to Europeans.
2. Despite a difficult beginning, the English colonies soon flourished.
3. In the mid-1700s, American colonists began to seek independence from British rule.

Key Terms and People

Paleo-Indians the first Americans who crossed from Asia into North America sometime between 38,000 and 10,000 BC

Christopher Columbus Italian explorer who was convinced that he could reach Asia by sailing westward across the Atlantic Ocean

Jamestown the first colony in the United States; set up in 1607 along the James River in Virginia

Puritans Protestants who wanted to reform the Church of England

Great Awakening a religious movement that became widespread in the American colonies in the 1730s and 1740s

Declaration of Independence the document written to declare the colonies free from British Rule

Patriots American colonists who fought for independence from Great Britain during the Revolutionary War

Treaty of Paris of 1783 a peace agreement that officially ended the Revolutionary War and established British recognition of the independence of the United States

Lesson Summary
AMERICAN BEGINNINGS

Some historians believe that **Paleo-Indians,** the first people to live in North America, came from Asia over the Bering Land Bridge. Others believe they traveled by boat. In time they formed many societies. Groups living along the Pacific Coast and in parts of the East and Southwest farmed,

How might Paleo-Indians from Asia have gotten to North America?

_____

_____

_____

_____

Guided Reading Workbook

hunted, and gathered plants. Others lived in areas that had few animals for hunting and were too dry or cold for farming. They moved often to find food. Some Native Americans built powerful empires. The Aztec and Maya built empires in Mexico, as did the Inca in Peru.

The Americas were isolated because of the Atlantic and Pacific Oceans. In the 1400s, Europeans wanted to find overseas routes to the valuable silk and spice trade in Asia. With Spain's support, **Christopher Columbus,** a sailor from Genoa, Italy, crossed the Atlantic Ocean in 1492. He did not land in Asia, but on an island in the Bahamas. Other Europeans followed. Spanish soldiers conquered the Aztec and Inca and took their lands, and Spain built an empire in the Americas. Then France, the Netherlands, and England began forming their own colonies, too.

THE ENGLISH COLONIES

The first English colony, **Jamestown,** was founded in 1607. Many colonists hoped to find wealth and opportunity. Some colonists who founded other colonies wanted religious freedom. Over time, England had thirteen colonies spread out in three different regions.

Settlers in the southern colonies grew cash crops such as tobacco and rice. Plantations used indentured servants and, later, enslaved Africans for labor.

The New England colonies were settled by **Puritans,** members of a religious group that had been persecuted in England. Puritans called Pilgrims landed at Plymouth Rock in present-day Massachusetts. Before leaving their ship, the male passengers signed the Mayflower Compact.

> Underline the sentence that tells the causes for some Native Americans having to move often to find food.

> What happened as a result of Columbus's voyage?
> _____
> _____
> _____
> _____
> _____

> Why did colonists come to the Americas?
> _____
> _____
> _____
> _____

> Why do you think the southern colonies relied on indentured servants and enslaved people?
> _____
> _____
> _____
> _____
> _____
> _____
> _____

Guided Reading Workbook

It established a self-governing colony based on majority rule of male church members. Only church members could vote or hold office. Town meetings were held to discuss issues, but conflicts over religious beliefs led Puritan leaders to banish people. These settlers built an economy based on shipping, fishing, farming, and manufacturing.

New York, New Jersey, Pennsylvania, and Delaware were the middle colonies. Similar to New England, they had towns that were centers of trade. Like the southern colonies, they grew crops such as wheat, barley, and oats. They mainly used indentured servants and some slaves for labor.

> Underline the sentence that tells the significance of the Mayflower Compact.

CREATING A NATION

The British colonies were spread apart and had little in common. However, the **Great Awakening,** a religious movement, and the French and Indian War helped unite them. The British won the war against France, and then Parliament began taxing colonial goods. The colonists resented this "taxation without representation." They boycotted British goods, which led to conflicts such as the Boston Massacre. After colonists dumped British tea into Boston Harbor, the city was occupied by British troops.

The colonists held the First Continental Congress and prepared for war. British troops set out to destroy supplies at Lexington and Concord, and colonial minutemen fought back in the first battles of the Revolutionary War. George Washington became head of the Continental Army.

> Underline the locations of the first battles of the Revolutionary War.

Thomas Paine's pamphlet *Common Sense* argued that the colonies declare independence. On July 4, 1776, the Continental Congress approved the **Declaration of Independence.** It said the colonists were free from British rule.

American colonists fighting for independence, the Patriots, had few victories at first. However, after they defeated the British in the Battle of Saratoga, France and Spain supported the **Patriots**. Eventually, Great Britain was forced to accept U.S. independence in the **Treaty of Paris of 1783**, which ended the Revolutionary War.

> **Why was the Battle of Saratoga important?**
> _____
> _____
> _____
> _____
> _____

CHALLENGE ACTIVITY

Critical Thinking: Evaluate Imagine that you lived in one of the thirteen colonies. Write a short paragraph describing why you settled there, how your life changed, and what you thought about the war.

DIRECTIONS Match the definition in the first column with the letter of the correct term in the second column.

_____ 1. American colonists who fought for independence from Great Britain

    a. Great Awakening

_____ 2. Italian explorer who was convinced that he could reach Asia by sailing westward across the Atlantic Ocean

    b. Jamestown

_____ 3. the first Americans who crossed from Asia into North America sometime between 38,000 and 10,000 BC

    c. Declaration of Independence

_____ 4. a peace agreement that officially ended the Revolutionary War and established British recognition of the independence of the United States

    d. Patriots

_____ 5. a religious movement that became widespread in the American colonies in the 1730s and 1740s

    e. Treaty of Paris of 1783

_____ 6. Protestants who wanted to reform the Church of England

    f. Paleo-Indians

_____ 7. the document written to declare the colonies free from British rule

    g. Christopher Columbus

_____ 8. the first colony in the United States, which was set up in 1607 along the James River in Virginia

    h. Puritans

U.S. History to 1860

MAIN IDEAS
1. The American people explored and tested many ideas to strengthen their government.
2. A new Constitution provided a framework for a stronger national government.
3. George Washington and members of Congress established a new national government.

Key Terms and People

Articles of Confederation the document that created the first central government for the United States

Shays's Rebellion an uprising of Massachusetts's farmers against the state court, led by Daniel Shays, to protest high taxes

Constitutional Convention a meeting held in Philadelphia at which delegates from the states wrote the Constitution

Three-Fifths Compromise an agreement stating that only three-fifths of a state's slaves would count when deciding representation in Congress

Antifederalists people who opposed ratification of the Constitution

Federalists people who supported ratification of the Constitution

federalism U.S. system of government in which power is distributed between a central government and individual states

George Washington Revolutionary War hero who commanded the Continental Army and was the first U.S. president

Lesson Summary
FORMING A GOVERNMENT

After winning independence, the United States needed a government. Americans used the English Bill of Rights, the Magna Carta, and the ideas of Enlightenment philosophers as models. They also had their own models, such as town meetings, the Mayflower Compact, and ideas from the Declaration of Independence. This led them to draft the **Articles of Confederation,** the document that created the first central government for the country. Congress had limited powers, and there was no executive branch or

> Underline models of government from the early history of the United States that leaders used when drafting the Articles of Confederation.

judicial system. The Congress did pass the Northwest Ordinance of 1787, allowing new territories to join the nation as equal states.

The Congress created by the Articles of Confederation was too weak to solve economic problems or make agreements with other nations. Great Britain and Spain cut off trade with American merchants and made them pay high taxes on imports and exports. Each state could make its own trade agreements and print its own money. War debt led some states to print too much money. The money became worthless and caused inflation. In Massachusetts, some poor farmers could not pay their high taxes on land. They protested against the state courts in an action that was known as **Shays's Rebellion**. This rebellion failed, but people realized that a change in government was needed.

The states sent delegates to a **Constitutional Convention** to make the Articles stronger. Instead, they wrote the U.S. Constitution. At the convention, there were many disputes between large and small states as well as northern and southern states. The delegates had to compromise. The Great Compromise gave every state an equal voice in the Senate and larger states more representation in the House of Representatives. The **Three-Fifths Compromise** counted three-fifths of the slave population when determining representation. Even with compromises, **Antifederalists** opposed the Constitution. Supporters of the document were called **Federalists**.

THE CONSTITUTION

The Constitution established a system of government called **federalism**. This system is one of the Constitution's strengths. It divides power between the states and the federal government.

> **What were three weaknesses of the Articles of Confederation?**
> _____
> _____
> _____
> _____
> _____
> _____
> _____

> **What happened as a result of Shays's Rebellion?**
> _____
> _____
> _____
> _____

> **Which compromises settled disputes at the Constitutional Convention?**
> _____
> _____
> _____

> **Underline the sentence that explains the system of government established by the Constitution.**

　Guided Reading Workbook

The Constitution also divided the powers of the federal government among three branches. The legislative branch, or Congress, passes laws. The executive branch, made up of the president and many departments, makes sure the laws are carried out. The judicial branch, or courts, interprets laws and punishes criminals. Through a system of checks and balances, no one branch can become too powerful. The Constitution also allows for amendments, or changes, to be made to adjust for changing times. To make sure this system works well, citizens have to fulfill their rights and responsibilities.

> **How is the Constitution able to stay current?**
> _____
> _____
> _____
> _____

WASHINGTON'S PRESIDENCY

After the Constitution was agreed to, Americans elected **George Washington** as their first U.S. president. Voters saw him as honest and as a hero of the Revolution. Congress created cabinet departments in the executive branch for different areas of national policy.

> **Underline the reasons George Washington became the first U.S. president.**

Thomas Jefferson became Secretary of State and Alexander Hamilton became Secretary of the Treasury. The two men disagreed about the size and purpose of government, how to finance it, and the interpretation of the Constitution.

The new government was not without problems. Washington faced conflicts at home and with other nations. While the United States remained neutral in European conflicts, the U.S. Army fought with Native Americans in the Northwest Territory. Also, after Congress passed a tax on American whiskey, angry farmers protested in the Whiskey Rebellion. Washington had to send an army to end the rebellion.

George Washington served as president for two terms and decided not to run again. In his Farewell Address to the nation, Washington warned against political parties and getting involved in foreign affairs.

> **How do you know that George Washington was in favor of neutrality?**
> _____
> _____
> _____
> _____
> _____
> _____
> _____

CHALLENGE ACTIVITY

Critical Thinking: Sequence Research events in this lesson to find when each one occurred. Create a timeline. Describe each event and explain how one event caused or affected another event. Illustrate your timeline.

DIRECTIONS Read each sentence. Choose which of the pair of answers given best completes the sentence and fill in the blank.

1. _____ was an uprising of Massachusetts's farmers against the state courts to protest high taxes. (Antifederalists/Shays's Rebellion)

2. The _____ was the meeting held in Philadelphia at which delegates from the states established our present system of government. (Constitutional Convention/Federalist Meeting)

3. The U.S. system of government in which power is distributed between the national government and individual states is known as _____. (federalism/Three-Fifths Compromise)

4. _____ were people who opposed the ratification of the Constitution. (Federalists/Antifederalists)

5. The Revolutionary War hero who commanded the Continental Army and was the first U.S. president was _____. (George Washington/Shays's Rebellion)

6. The _____ was an agreement stating how many of a state's slaves would count when deciding representation in Congress. (Three-Fifths Compromise/Constitutional Convention)

7. The document that created the first central government for the United States was the _____. (Constitutional Convention/Articles of Confederation)

8. People who supported ratification of the Constitution were _____. (George Washington/Federalists)

U.S. History to 1860

Lesson 3

> **MAIN IDEAS**
> 1. The presidential election of 1796 saw the rise of political parties and began a new era in U.S. politics.
> 2. Success in war contributed to a growing sense of American nationalism.
> 3. Jacksonian democracy was marked by an expansion of voting rights and a strong executive branch.

Key Terms and People

Thomas Jefferson American statesman; the Declaration of Independence's main author; the third U.S. president

Alien and Sedition Acts laws passed by a Federalist-dominated Congress that limited freedom of speech and the press

Louisiana Purchase the purchase of French land between the Mississippi River and the Rocky Mountains that nearly doubled the size of the United States

Lewis and Clark Expedition an expedition led by Meriwether Lewis and William Clark that began in 1804 to explore the Louisiana Purchase

Monroe Doctrine President James Monroe's statement warning European nations to stay out of affairs in the Western Hemisphere

Erie Canal the canal that runs from Albany to Buffalo, New York; completed in 1825

Missouri Compromise an agreement proposed by Henry Clay that allowed Missouri to enter the Union as a slave state and Maine to enter as a free state and outlawed slavery in any territories or states north of 36°30' latitude

Jacksonian Democracy an expansion of voting rights during the popular Andrew Jackson administration

Lesson Summary
THE AMERICAN REPUBLIC

In the 1796 presidential election, Federalist John Adams defeated Democratic-Republican **Thomas Jefferson,** Declaration of Independence author. When the country almost went to war with France, some Democratic-Republicans criticized Federalists. This led Congress to pass the **Alien and Sedition Acts,** which limited freedom of speech and the press.

> **Why did Congress pass the Alien and Sedition Acts?**
> _____
> _____
> _____
> _____
> _____

Jefferson and others said these acts were unconstitutional. Then in 1800, Jefferson beat Adams and became the third president. It was the first time in U.S. history that power changed from one political party to another.

Several important events occurred during Jefferson's presidency. In *Marbury* v. *Madison,* the Supreme Court increased its power by establishing judicial review, which allows the court to declare acts of Congress unconstitutional. Jefferson made the **Louisiana Purchase,** which gave the country land between the Mississippi River and the Rocky Mountains. It almost doubled the size of the country. Then he sent Meriwether Lewis and William Clark on the **Lewis and Clark Expedition**. They explored and mapped the Louisiana territory.

Maintaining neutrality with France and Great Britain was difficult during this time. The country could either ban trade with both countries, which would hurt Americans, or trade with both countries. The United States decided to trade. Both Spain and Britain captured U.S. ships that were on their way to trade with the other country. Also, Britain supported Native Americans who were against American settlement in the West. By this time James Madison was president. He called for war against Britain. Neither side gained any territory in the war, which was called the War of 1812.

GROWING NATIONALISM

Success from the War of 1812 led to an increase in American patriotism, and President Monroe issued the **Monroe Doctrine**. It warned Europeans to stay out of affairs in the Western Hemisphere.

Between 1815 and 1825, known as the Era of Good Feelings, the country had little political conflict. Roads and canals were built to connect

| Underline the sentence that provides a reason why the 1800 election was important. |

| Why was the Louisiana Purchase important for the United States?
_____
_____
_____
_____
_____ |

| Why do you think Britain might have supported Native Americans who were against American settlement in the West?
_____
_____
_____
_____
_____
_____ |

| What was the purpose of the Monroe Doctrine?
_____
_____
_____
_____ |

distant regions. One canal, the **Erie Canal,** ran from Albany to Buffalo, New York. Also, writers and painters created new American styles of literature and art. There was a feeling of nationalism, or pride in country.

However, one threat continued to be an issue to the country's unity. States in the North and South disagreed about the expansion of slavery westward. The **Missouri Compromise** of 1820 was a temporary solution to the problem. It tried to maintain the balance between the number of slave and free states.

> **During the Era of Good Feelings, what was a threat to unity in the United States?**
>
> _____
>
> _____

THE AGE OF JACKSON

Andrew Jackson was defeated in the 1824 presidential election. After that, his supporters created the Democratic Party. By 1828 many states had laws that increased voting rights for white men. This became known as **Jacksonian Democracy** after Andrew Jackson. When Jackson won the 1828 presidential election, many people thought it was a victory for the common people.

During Jackson's presidency, South Carolina said it would leave the country if Congress did not lower taxes on imports. Jackson did not believe that states should have the power to reject laws made by Congress. South Carolina did not leave the country. However, Jackson himself did not always follow federal authority. For example, when the Supreme Court said the Second Bank of the United States was constitutional in *McCulloch* v. *Maryland,* Jackson opposed the ruling and worked to end public support for it. Jackson's refusal to follow the Supreme Court's decision led to an economic depression known as the Panic of 1837. By then Jackson was no longer president. And, in the 1840 presidential election, the Democratic Party lost to the Whig Party.

> **How did Jacksonian Democracy help Andrew Jackson win the 1828 presidential election?**
>
> _____
>
> _____
>
> _____
>
> _____
>
> _____
>
> _____

> **What was the effect of Jackson's refusal to follow the Supreme Court's decision in *McCulloch* v. *Maryland*?**
>
> _____
>
> _____
>
> _____
>
> _____
>
> _____
>
> _____
>
> _____

CHALLENGE ACTIVITY

Critical Thinking: Compare and Contrast Write a short essay comparing and contrasting the presidencies of Jefferson and Jackson. Use specific examples that demonstrate how they affected the United States.

DIRECTIONS Write two adjectives or descriptive phrases that
describe the term, person, or event.

1. Thomas Jefferson _____

_____

2. Louisiana Purchase _____

_____

3. Jacksonian Democracy _____

_____

4. Erie Canal _____

_____

5. Alien and Sedition Acts _____

_____

6. Missouri Compromise _____

_____

7. Monroe Doctrine _____

_____

8. Lewis and Clark Expedition _____

_____

Lesson 4

MAIN IDEAS
1. Westward expansion transformed the nation.
2. The Industrial Revolution transformed life in the northern states.
3. The Southern economy and society centered on agriculture.
4. In the mid-1800s, social reformers aimed to improve lives of Americans.

Key Terms and People

Trail of Tears an 800-mile forced march made by the Cherokee westward in which almost one-fourth of the Cherokee people died

Oregon Trail a 2,000-mile trail stretching through the Great Plains from western Missouri to the Oregon Territory

manifest destiny a belief shared by many Americans in the mid-1800s that the United States should expand across the continent to the Pacific Ocean

Eli Whitney an American inventor whose cotton gin enabled large increases in cotton production

abolition movement a campaign to end slavery

Frederick Douglass American abolitionist and writer who escaped slavery and became a leading African American spokesperson

temperance movement a social reform effort begun in the mid-1800s to encourage people to drink less alcohol

Elizabeth Cady Stanton American woman suffrage leader who helped organize the Seneca Falls Convention; co-founder of the National Woman Suffrage Association

Lesson Summary
EXPANDING WEST

During the 1800s, thousands of Native Americans lived on land east of the Mississippi River. In 1830, Congress passed the Indian Removal Act, which allowed the United States to move them to western land known as Indian Territory. The Cherokee protested the law, and the Supreme Court ruled in their favor. However, it did no good, and in 1838 the Cherokee were forced to march on the 800-mile **Trail of Tears.** Thousands of Cherokee died.

> **Why do you think the United States passed the Indian Removal Act?**
>
> _____
> _____
> _____
> _____

The U.S. population had increased during the 1800s. Many settlers moved westward beyond the country's boundaries. Thousands of pioneers followed the 2,000-mile-long **Oregon Trail** to the Pacific Northwest. Thousands of others settled in Texas, a Mexican province. Mexico's government banned further American settlement since it believed Americans were not following Mexican laws. This led to a Texas rebellion in 1836 and Texan independence.

Many Americans believed that they had the right to settle all the way to the Pacific Ocean. This was known as **manifest destiny.** They wanted to annex Texas and Oregon. President Polk gained Oregon through a treaty with Great Britain. However, the conflict over Texas led to the Mexican-American War. The U.S. won and gained more land, including California and most of the present-day American Southwest. When gold was discovered in California, many miners moved to the territory. Because California's population and economy grew, by 1850 California became the 31st state.

> **What were two effects of manifest destiny?**
> _____
> _____
> _____
> _____
> _____
> _____
> _____

> **Underline the sentence that tells what happened as a result of the discovery of gold in California and an influx of miners into the territory.**

THE INDUSTRIAL NORTH

Westward movement was not the only expansion in the United States. New industries grew in the Northeast. Factories made cloth using water-powered machines. **Eli Whitney,** the inventor of the cotton gin, developed the idea of interchangeable parts. This led to mass production.

Factories moved to cities. City populations grew quickly thanks to new factory jobs and the arrival of millions of immigrants. There was a new middle class of managers and skilled workers. The rapid growth caused overcrowding, crime, and disease.

Transportation and communication improved during the mid-1800s, which improved the

> **What factors contributed to the growth of cities?**
> _____
> _____
> _____
> _____

economy. Steamboats and steam-powered trains made transportation faster and cheaper. The telegraph carried messages across wires.

THE AGRICULTURAL SOUTH

While the North was industrial and had big cities, the South was rural and agricultural. It relied on cash crops and attracted fewer immigrants. The South's main crops were originally tobacco, rice, and indigo. Then, with Eli Whitney's cotton gin, cotton became the South's largest crop. Demand for cotton was great due to the large number of textile mills in the North and in Great Britain. The South became important in the world trade market.

Cotton brought wealth to the South, and it increased the need for slave labor. Many slaves lived on large plantations owned by wealthy planters. They received harsh treatment and their living conditions were poor.

> Underline the sentence that tells how the North and South were different.

> What was a positive effect of cotton and a negative effect?
> _____
> _____
> _____
> _____
> _____

NEW MOVEMENTS IN SOCIETY

In opposition to slavery, some Americans formed the **abolition movement.** Two leading abolitionists were former slaves **Frederick Douglass** and Sojourner Truth. Abolitionists spread their antislavery messages through speeches and newspapers.

Another reform movement was the **temperance movement,** which wanted to stop alcohol abuse. Some reformers worked for better treatment for prisoners. Others involved education reform. People wanted more public schools for children as well as educational opportunities for African Americans and women.

Some women, such as **Elizabeth Cady Stanton,** began to demand more rights for women, including women's suffrage, or the right to vote. These fights were the beginning of gaining equal right for many Americans.

> Which reform movement was in opposition to slavery?
> _____

> Underline the cause Elizabeth Cady Stanton fought for.

Guided Reading Workbook

CHALLENGE ACTIVITY

Critical Thinking: Cause and Effect Make a chart
identifying at least three cause-and-effect
relationships from the lesson.

abolition movement	Frederick Douglass	temperance movement
Eli Whitney	manifest destiny	Trail of Tears
Elizabeth Cady Stanton	Oregon Trail	

DIRECTIONS Answer each question by writing a sentence that
contains at least one term or person from the word bank.

1. What social reform effort was meant to encourage people to drink less?

   _____

2. On which trail did people travel through the Great Plains from western
   Missouri to the Pacific Northwest? _____

   _____

3. Which former slave was a leading American abolitionist? _____

   _____

4. Who fought for women's rights, including women's suffrage?

   _____

5. What belief made many Americans think the United States should expand
   across the continent to the Pacific Ocean? _____

   _____

   _____

6. Who invented the cotton gin and developed the idea of
   interchangeable parts? _____

   _____

7. What was the forced march westward made by the Cherokee known as?

   _____

   _____

8. Which reform movement campaigned to end slavery? _____

   _____

U.S. History to 1860

MAIN IDEAS

1. By the mid-1800s, the nation was deeply divided by the issue of slavery.
2. Political division and judicial decisions increased the debate over slavery.

Key Terms and People

Free-Soil Party a political party formed in 1848 to oppose the spread of slavery

Compromise of 1850 Henry Clay's proposed agreement that allowed California to enter the Union as a free state, but gave other territories in the Southwest the choice as to whether to allow slavery

Fugitive Slave Act a law that made it a crime to help runaway slaves

Kansas-Nebraska Act a law that allowed voters in Kansas and Nebraska to choose whether to allow slavery

Harriet Beecher Stowe American author of the antislavery novel *Uncle Tom's Cabin*

Dred Scott Enslaved man who filed suit for his freedom, resulting in a Supreme Court ruling that African Americans could not be citizens and that Congress could not ban slavery in any of the territories

Abraham Lincoln sixteenth president of the United States

Confederate States of America the nation formed by the southern states when they seceded from the Union; also known as the Confederacy

Lesson Summary
DEEPENING DIVISIONS

The North and South had many differences, including their economies, societies, and goals. Many northerners did not want slavery to spread to the West and proposed a ban. Southerners opposed this idea. A new political party arose in the North, which opposed the spread of slavery. It was the **Free-Soil Party.**

When California was to become a state, its status as a slave or free state threatened the political balance of the Senate. Henry Clay offered the **Compromise of 1850.** It said that

> **What was the problem related to statehood for California ?**
>
> _____
> _____
> _____
> _____

California could join as a free state, but other Southwest territories would be able to choose whether to allow slavery. With this compromise came the **Fugitive Slave Act.** This law made it easier to capture runaway slaves and angered many northerners. **The Kansas-Nebraska Act** also upset those opposed to slavery because it made the spread of slavery possible in Kansas and Nebraska. And with the writing of the popular antislavery novel, *Uncle Tom's Cabin*, author **Harriet Beecher Stowe** upset many southerners. So when the Kansas Territory was opened, those in favor of and those against slavery went to the territory hoping to gain control. The groups clashed and a series of attacks and killings in Kansas shocked the nation.

Why did the Fugitive Slave Act and the Kansas-Nebraska Act upset those opposed to slavery?
_____ _____ _____ _____ _____ _____ _____

Underline the novel written by Harriet Beecher Stowe that upset many southerners.

PRELUDE TO WAR

Then the Supreme Court got involved and shocked northerners. In a case involving an enslaved man named **Dred Scott**, the Court ruled that African Americans could not be citizens and that Congress could not ban slavery. Then the South got a shock when abolitionist John Brown tried to start a slave rebellion by attacking Harpers Ferry, Virginia.

In the midst of all this turmoil, the presidential election of 1860 took place. Republican **Abraham Lincoln** won; however, he did not receive a single electoral vote from the South.

Southern leaders thought that Lincoln would ban slavery, which would destroy the South's economy. Seven states—South Carolina, Mississippi, Florida, Alabama, Georgia, Louisiana, and Texas—left the Union. They formed the **Confederate States of America,** or the Confederacy. Lincoln said that the states could not simply leave. The stage was set for a terrible civil war between the North and the South.

What ruling did the Supreme Court make regarding slavery?
_____ _____ _____ _____ _____

Why did seven states leave the Union?
_____ _____ _____

CHALLENGE ACTIVITY
Critical Thinking: Make Inferences Henry Clay continued to propose compromises to deal with the disagreement over slavery. Write a short essay in which you explain why compromises did not solve the problem.

Abraham Lincoln	Dred Scott	Harriet Beecher Stowe
Compromise of 1850	Free-Soil Party	Kansas-Nebraska Act
Confederate States of America	Fugitive Slave Act	

DIRECTIONS Use the eight vocabulary words above to write a summary of what you learned in the lesson.

_____

_____

_____

_____

_____

_____

_____

_____

_____

_____

_____

Lesson 1

MAIN IDEAS
1. Following the outbreak of war at Fort Sumter, Americans chose sides.
2. The Union and the Confederacy prepared for war.

Key Terms and People

Fort Sumter federal post in Charleston, South Carolina, that surrendered to the Confederacy; marked the beginning of the Civil War

border states four slave states—Delaware, Kentucky, Maryland, and Missouri—that bordered the North and did not join the Confederacy

Winfield Scott Union general with a two-part strategy for defeating the Confederacy

cotton diplomacy Confederate plan to enlist Britain's aid in return for continued cotton shipments

Lesson Summary
AMERICANS CHOOSE SIDES

After being elected in 1860, Abraham Lincoln took office as seven southern states left the Union. He promised he would not end slavery where it existed. However, he also promised to preserve the Union.

Confederate officials already were taking control of federal mints, arsenals, and forts. Fighting finally broke out at **Fort Sumter**, a federal fort in the Confederate state of South Carolina. Federal troops refused to surrender to the Confederacy. Within two days, Fort Sumter fell. Lincoln called for 75,000 militiamen to put down the South's rebellion.

After Lincoln called for troops, all the states had to choose a side. Four more slave states joined the Confederacy. Four **border states**—slave states that bordered the North—decided to stay in the Union. In addition, western Virginia broke

How did the South react to Lincoln's election to the presidency?

_____

_____

How did Lincoln respond to the surrender of Fort Sumter?

_____

_____

off from Confederate Virginia to stay in the Union.

Union general **Winfield Scott** had a two-part strategy to conquer the South. First, he would destroy the South's economy with a naval blockade of southern ports. Second, Scott would gain control of the Mississippi River, which would help divide the South.

The Confederacy had its own plan of attack. Part of that plan involved **cotton diplomacy**—the hope that Britain would support the Confederacy because it needed Confederate cotton. This strategy did not work because Britain had large stores of cotton and got more from India and Egypt.

> **Why didn't cotton diplomacy work?**
> _____
> _____

PREPARING FOR WAR

Neither side was prepared for the war to come. However, many citizens—northern and southern— were eager to help. Thousands upon thousands of young men answered the call to arms and volunteered to serve in both armies.

Civilians, too, volunteered to help. They raised money to aid soldiers and their families. They staffed and supplied emergency hospitals. In the Union alone, about 3,000 women served as army nurses.

> **In what ways did civilians help the war effort?**
> _____
> _____
> _____

Once the thousands of farmers, teachers, laborers, and others joined the armies, they had to be trained to become soldiers. They spent long days drilling and practicing with their guns and bayonets. As a result, many young soldiers were ready to fight.

CHALLENGE ACTIVITY

Critical Thinking: Design Write an advertisement encouraging people to support the soldiers by coming to a fundraising event.

Lesson 1, *continued*

Abraham Lincoln	cotton diplomacy	Winfield Scott
border states	Fort Sumter	

DIRECTIONS Use the five vocabulary words from the word list to write a summary of what you learned in the lesson.

_____

_____

_____

_____

_____

_____

_____

_____

_____

_____

DIRECTIONS Read each sentence and fill in the blank with the word in the word pair that best completes the sentence.

1. The Civil War began in 1861 when Confederate troops began to fire on _____. (border states/Fort Sumter)

2. Union general _____ planned to destroy the South's economy with a naval blockade of southern ports. (Abraham Lincoln/ Winfield Scott)

3. The South tried to win foreign allies through _____. (border states/cotton diplomacy)

4. In his inaugural address, _____ promised not to end slavery where it existed. (Abraham Lincoln/Winfield Scott)

5. Delaware, Kentucky, Maryland, and Missouri were _____ that did not join the Confederacy. (border states/cotton diplomacy)

Guided Reading Workbook

The Civil War

MAIN IDEAS
1. Union and Confederate forces fought for control of the war in Virginia.
2. The Battle of Antietam gave the North a slight advantage.
3. The Confederacy attempted to break the Union naval blockade.

Key Terms and People

Thomas "Stonewall" Jackson Confederate general who helped fight Union troops at the First Battle of Bull Run

First Battle of Bull Run battle near Manassas Junction, Virginia, in 1861

George B. McClellan general sent by President Lincoln to capture Richmond

Robert E. Lee Confederate general during many important battles of the Civil War

Seven Days' Battles series of battles that forced McClellan to retreat from near Richmond

Second Battle of Bull Run Confederate attack that helped push Union forces out of Virginia

Battle of Antietam battle in Maryland that resulted in Lee's retreat to Virginia

ironclads ships that were heavily armored with iron

Lesson Summary

WAR IN VIRGINIA

In July 1861 the Union and Confederate armies clashed near Manassas Junction, Virginia, along Bull Run Creek. At first the Union soldiers, under General Irvin McDowell, pushed back the left side of the Confederate line. Then southern troops, led by General **Thomas "Stonewall" Jackson**, fought back. With reinforcements arriving, the Confederate troops drove the Union army back. This conflict was called the **First Battle of Bull Run**. It showed that the war would not be an easy victory for the Union.

After the failed attempt to take Richmond, Lincoln tried again. This time he sent new commander General **George B. McClellan**. In the

> **What did the First Battle of Bull Run show?**
> _____
> _____

spring of 1862 McClellan led 100,000 soldiers, called the Army of the Potomac, on a slow march to Richmond.

Then, in June, General **Robert E. Lee** took command of the Confederate forces. On June 26 the two armies met in the **Seven Days' Battles**. These battles pushed McClellan away from Richmond. Lee saved Richmond and forced McClellan to retreat. Then during the **Second Battle of Bull Run**, Jackson's troops defeated another Union army before it could march directly on Richmond.

> Underline all the Civil War battles identified on this page.

BATTLE OF ANTIETAM

A copy of Lee's battle strategy left behind led to the next major battle of the Civil War. The Union discovered the Confederates were going to attack Harpers Ferry. McClellan sent his troops to stop them. The two armies met along Antietam Creek in Maryland. The **Battle of Antietam** took place on September 17, 1862. It halted Lee's northward march. This battle was a success. However, it was the bloodiest single-day battle of the Civil War and of United States history. The Union suffered more than 12,000 casualties and the Confederates suffered more than 13,000 casualties.

BREAKING THE UNION'S BLOCKADE

Despite the distance it had to control, the Union blockade of southern ports was very effective. It reduced the number of ships entering southern ports from 6,000 to 800 per year. Both sides had the innovation of **ironclads**. However, the Union continued the blockade unbroken.

> Underline the sentence that supports the statement that the Union blockade of southern ports was very effective.

CHALLENGE ACTIVITY

Critical Thinking: Explain How was a mistake responsible for the Battle of Antietam?

Guided Reading Workbook

Battle of Antietam	ironclads	Seven Days' Battles
First Battle of Bull Run	Robert E. Lee	Thomas "Stonewall" Jackson
George B. McClellan	Second Battle of Bull Run	

DIRECTIONS Use five of the terms or names from the word bank to write a letter that relates to the lesson.

Dear _____

_____

_____

_____

_____

_____

_____

_____

_____

_____

_____

DIRECTIONS On the line provided before each statement, write **T** if a statement is true and **F** if a statement is false. If the statement is false, write the correct term on the line after each sentence that makes the sentence a true statement.

_____ 1. General <u>George B. McClellan</u> commanded the Confederate forces during the Seven Days' Battles. He saved Richmond and forced the Union army to retreat.

_____

_____ 2. The <u>Battle of Antietam</u> was the bloodiest single-day battle of the Civil War, with a total of more than 25,000 casualties.

_____

Lesson 2, *continued*

_____ 3. The North's hopes of winning the war quickly and easily were crushed when the Union army was defeated at the <u>Second Battle of Bull Run</u>.

_____

_____ 4. General <u>Thomas "Stonewall" Jackson</u> led Confederate troops to victory during the First Battle of Bull Run.

_____

The Civil War

Lesson 3

> **MAIN IDEAS**
> 1. Union strategy in the West centered on control of the Mississippi River.
> 2. Confederate and Union troops struggled for dominance in the Far West.

Key Terms and People

Ulysses S. Grant Union general whose troops won several important battles on southern soil and in the western campaign

Battle of Shiloh battle in which Union troops gained greater control of the Mississippi River valley

David Farragut naval leader who helped the Union take control of New Orleans

Siege of Vicksburg six-week blockade of Vicksburg that starved the city into surrender

Lesson Summary

UNION STRATEGY IN THE WEST

In February 1862 General **Ulysses S. Grant** led a Union army into Tennessee. He was headed toward the Mississippi River. He wanted to capture outposts that would separate the eastern Confederacy from its western, food-supplying states. On the way Grant and his forces took both Fort Henry and Fort Donelson.

Near Shiloh Church, Grant halted his troops to wait for more soldiers to arrive. Grant was aware of Confederate troops in the area. However, he was caught by surprise when they attacked on April 6. During the two-day **Battle of Shiloh**, each side lost and gained ground. Union reinforcements arrived. They helped push the Confederates into retreating. This win helped the Union control part of the Mississippi River valley.

To control the Mississippi River, the Union had to first deal with New Orleans. This was the South's largest city and the valuable port near the

> **Why did the Union consider control of the Mississippi River critical?**
> _____
> _____
> _____

> **How do you know that Fort Henry and Fort Donelson were Confederate forts?**
> _____
> _____

mouth of the Mississippi River. However, two forts guarded New Orleans from the south.

Union admiral **David Farragut** solved that problem. He disguised his boats and raced past the two forts in the darkness before dawn on April 24, 1862. Within days New Orleans fell to the Union troops. Farragut continued north, taking more cities, until he reached Vicksburg, Mississippi.

Vicksburg was located on cliffs high above the Mississippi River. This allowed Confederate general John C. Pemberton to stop any attempt to attack the city. So, instead of trying to attack Vicksburg directly, General Grant cut the city off. He shelled it repeatedly. The **Siege of Vicksburg** lasted about six weeks before hunger forced the Confederates to surrender. The Mississippi River was now under Union control.

STRUGGLE FOR THE FAR WEST

The Confederates tried to take control of the southwest. So fighting also broke out there.

Defeats in Arizona and at Glorieta Pass stopped Confederates from taking lands in the West. Confederate-Union conflicts in Missouri also ended with a Confederate defeat. This was despite aid from the Cherokee. Attacks on Union forts and raids on towns forced the Union commanders to keep valuable troops stationed in the western states and territories.

CHALLENGE ACTIVITY

Critical Thinking: Analyze Write a paragraph analyzing why the Union wanted to control the West.

How was New Orleans captured?
_____
_____
_____

Why was Vicksburg difficult to capture?
_____
_____
_____

Why did the Siege of Vicksburg succeed when attacks on Vicksburg had failed?
_____
_____
_____

Lesson 3, *continued*

| Battle of Shiloh | John C. Pemberton | Ulysses S. Grant |
| David Farragut | Siege of Vicksburg | |

DIRECTIONS Answer each question by writing a sentence that contains at least one word from the word bank.

1. Which Union commander was the most important figure in the war in the West?

_____

_____

2. Who was the Union naval leader from Tennessee who captured New Orleans?

_____

_____

3. What is the name of the event where the Union army, under General Ulysses S. Grant, gained greater control of the Mississippi River?

_____

_____

4. Who was the Confederate general who attempted to defend the city of Vicksburg, Mississippi, from Union attack?

_____

_____

5. What event lasted about six weeks and ended when the Union captured Vicksburg, Mississippi?

_____

_____

Guided Reading Workbook

MAIN IDEAS
1. The Emancipation Proclamation freed slaves in Confederate states.
2. African Americans participated in the war in a variety of ways.
3. President Lincoln faced opposition to the war.
4. Life was difficult for soldiers and civilians alike.

Key Terms and People

emancipation the freeing of slaves

Emancipation Proclamation order to free Confederate slaves

contrabands escaped slaves

54th Massachusetts Infantry heroic unit of mostly free African American soldiers

Copperheads nickname for the Peace Democrats, a group who spoke out against the war

habeas corpus constitutional protection against unlawful imprisonment

Clara Barton army volunteer whose work was basis for the American Red Cross

Lesson Summary
EMANCIPATION PROCLAMATION

President Lincoln realized that one way to weaken the South was to free the slaves. **Emancipation** would free many slaves on which the South's economy relied. After the Battle of Antietam, Lincoln presented the **Emancipation Proclamation**. Despite the impossibility of enforcing it in Confederate-held states, the proclamation still had a distinct effect on the war.

> What was the purpose of the Emancipation Proclamation?
>
> _____
> _____
> _____

AFRICAN AMERICANS PARTICIPATE IN THE WAR

In July 1862 Congress decided to allow African Americans to join the army as laborers. This decision included both free African Americans and **contrabands**, or escaped slaves. Within a year several African American units had formed. The most famous unit was the **54th Massachusetts**

> How were contrabands different from other African Americans who joined the Union army?
>
> _____
> _____
> _____

Infantry. These troops helped attack South
Carolina's Fort Wagner.

African American soldiers received less pay
than white soldiers. They also faced greater
danger. If captured by Confederates, they could
be returned to slavery. In fact, Lincoln suggested
these soldiers be rewarded by getting the right to
vote.

GROWING OPPOSITION

Some midwesterners and northerners did not
think the war was necessary. They called
themselves Peace Democrats, but their enemies
called them **Copperheads**, after the poisonous
snake.

Lincoln saw Copperheads as a threat to the
war effort. Because of this, he had Copperheads
put in jail with no evidence and no trial. To do
this, he ignored their right of **habeas corpus**. This
is constitutional protection against unlawful
imprisonment. Despite this and the northern
draft, Lincoln won his second election in 1864.

> **What is habeas corpus?**
> _____
> _____

LIFE FOR SOLDIERS AND CIVILIANS

For the soldier, both camp life and combat
offered dangers. Poor camp conditions, including
lack of medicine and painkillers, led to illness.
This alone killed more men than battle did.
Those wounded or captured in battle often met
the same fate.

Those left behind took over the work of the
men who went to war. In addition, many women
also provided medical care for the soldiers. For
example, volunteer **Clara Barton** collected
medicine and supplies for the Union troops. Her
work led to the forming of the organization that
would become the American Red Cross.

> **How did women help the war effort?**
> _____
> _____
> _____

CHALLENGE ACTIVITY

Critical Thinking: Contrast First, imagine you are a lawyer for the Peace Democrats. Write a paragraph explaining why the right of habeas corpus should not be ignored. Then imagine you are a lawyer for the federal government. Write a paragraph defending Lincoln's actions.

DIRECTIONS Read each sentence and fill in the blank with the word in the word pair that best completes the sentence.

1. The _____ called for all Confederate slaves to be freed. (habeas corpus/Emancipation Proclamation)

2. The _____ consisted mostly of free African Americans. (Emancipation Proclamation/54th Massachusetts Infantry)

3. _____ were a group of Northern Democrats who spoke out against the Civil War. (Contrabands/Copperheads)

4. _____ is the constitutional protection against unlawful imprisonment. (Habeas corpus/Emancipation)

5. _____ volunteered during the Civil War and organized the collection of medicine and supplies for delivery to Union troops on the battlefield. (Clara Barton/Copperheads)

6. The War Department gave _____, or escaped slaves, the right to join the Union army. (contrabands/Copperheads)

7. _____ is the freeing of slaves. (Habeas corpus/ Emancipation)

8. More soldiers died from _____. (poor camp conditons/ lack of medicine)

9. African American soldiers faced greater danger because they could be _____ if captured. (imprisoned/returned to slavery)

10. Although they faced greater danger, African American soldiers received _____. (the right to vote/less pay)

The Civil War

Lesson 5

MAIN IDEAS
1. The Union tried to divide the Confederate army at Fredericksburg, but the attempt failed.
2. The Battle of Gettysburg in 1863 was a major turning point in the war.
3. During 1864, Union campaigns in the East and South dealt crippling blows to the Confederacy.
4. Union troops forced the South to surrender in 1865, ending the Civil War.

Key Terms and People

Battle of Gettysburg three-day key battle that Confederates lost

George Pickett general who carried out Lee's orders to charge the Union line

Pickett's Charge disastrous attempt by Pickett's troops to storm Cemetery Ridge

Gettysburg Address speech in which Lincoln praised the bravery of Union soldiers and renewed his commitment to winning the war

Wilderness Campaign series of battles in which Grant tried to take Richmond

William Tecumseh Sherman Union general who cut a path of destruction across Georgia

total war strategy in which both civilian and military resources are destroyed

Appomattox Courthouse the place where Lee surrendered to Grant

Lesson Summary
FREDERICKSBURG AND CHANCELLORSVILLE
In late 1862 Confederate troops under the command of General Robert E. Lee won a battle at Fredericksburg, Virginia. In the spring of 1863 they again defeated Union troops at Chancellorsville.

BATTLE OF GETTYSBURG
Hoping a Confederate win on Union soil would break the Union's spirit, Lee headed into Union territory. The **Battle of Gettysburg**, which started July 1, 1863, was the consequence.

The first day, Lee's troops pushed Union general George G. Meade's soldiers back. The

> Why did the Battle of Gettysburg start?
> _____
> _____

Union troops had to dig in on top of two hills outside the town. On the second day, Confederate troops tried to take the hill called Little Round Top but failed. On the third day, Lee ordered General **George Pickett** to lead a charge on Cemetery Ridge. **Pickett's Charge** was a disaster. Over half the Confederates were killed, and Lee retreated. Never again would his troops reach northern land. The Battle of Gettysburg was the turning point in the war.

President Lincoln helped dedicate a new cemetery at Gettysburg. On November 19, 1863, he delivered the **Gettysburg Address**.

> **How long did the Battle of Gettysburg last?**
> _____
> _____

> **Who won the Battle of Gettysburg?**
> _____

UNION CAMPAIGNS CRIPPLE THE CONFEDERACY

The **Wilderness Campaign** was a series of battles fought in Virginia around Richmond. Although he lost more men than Lee, Grant also had more reinforcements. As a result of the battles, Grant was winning the war. However, at Petersburg, Lee's defenses did not allow Grant to execute his attack and capture Richmond.

To assure his reelection, Lincoln needed a victory. General **William Tecumseh Sherman** provided it by capturing Atlanta, Georgia. This victory helped Lincoln get reelected in a landslide.

Sherman did not stop at Atlanta. He ordered his troops to cut a path of destruction through Georgia, practicing **total war** all the way to the ocean.

> **How did General William Sherman help President Lincoln get reelected?**
> _____
> _____
> _____

THE SOUTH SURRENDERS

On April 9, 1865, at **Appomattox Courthouse**, Lee officially surrendered to Grant. The long, bloody war was over, but the question of how the United States could be united again remained.

> **In what year did the Civil War end?**
> _____

Lesson 5, *continued*

CHALLENGE ACTIVITY

Critical Thinking: Sequence Use dates and events
in this lesson to make a timeline of the Civil War.

Appomattox Courthouse	George Pickett	total war
Battle of Gettysburg	Gettysburg Address	Wilderness Campaign
George G. Meade	Pickett's Charge	William Tecumseh Sherman

DIRECTIONS On the line provided before each statement, write **T** if
a statement is true and **F** if a statement is false. If the statement is
false, write the correct term on the line after each sentence that
makes the sentence a true statement.

_____ 1. The <u>Battle of Gettysburg</u> was a turning point in the Civil War and
made northerners believe the war could be won.

_____

_____ 2. The Battle of Gettysburg began when Confederate soldiers raided the
city of Gettysburg and clashed with Union cavalry led by General
<u>George G. Meade</u>.

_____

_____ 3. <u>William Tecumseh Sherman</u> carried out General Lee's order to attack
the Union's line during the Battle of Gettysburg.

_____

_____ 4. Over half of the Confederate troops were killed in <u>total war</u>, which
was a disastrous attack on Union forces at Cemetery Ridge during the
Battle of Gettysburg.

_____

Guided Reading Workbook

_____ 5. The <u>Wilderness Campaign</u>, given at the dedication of the cemetery at the Gettysburg battlefield, was a short but moving speech, and is one of the most famous speeches in American history.

_____

_____ 6. <u>William Tecumseh Sherman</u> carried out a campaign, known as total war, to destroy southern railroads and industries to ruin the South's economy and its ability to fight.

_____

Lesson 1

> **MAIN IDEAS**
> 1. President Lincoln and Congress differed in their views as Reconstruction began.
> 2. The end of the Civil War meant freedom for African Americans in the South.
> 3. President Johnson's plan began the process of Reconstruction.

Key Terms and People

Reconstruction the process of readmitting the former Confederate states to the Union following the end of the Civil War

Ten Percent Plan Lincoln's Reconstruction plan, which required that 10 percent of voters in a state pledge loyalty to the United States before that state could rejoin the Union

Thirteenth Amendment the amendment that made slavery illegal throughout the United States

Freedmen's Bureau an organization established by Congress to provide relief for freedpeople and certain poor people in the South

Andrew Johnson vice president who became president upon Lincoln's death

Lesson Summary
RECONSTRUCTION BEGINS

As soon as the Civil War ended, Reconstruction began. **Reconstruction** was a period of reuniting the nation and rebuilding the southern states. The former Confederate states were readmitted to the union during this time.

President Lincoln proposed that southerners be offered amnesty, or an official pardon. Southerners had to swear an oath of loyalty to the United States and accept the ban on slavery. When 10 percent of the voters in any state took the oath, that state could be accepted back into the Union. This was called the **Ten Percent Plan**.

Some supported the Wade-Davis Bill instead. The Wade-Davis Bill required southerners to ban slavery. However, under this bill, most of the people of a state would have to take the pledge before the state could rejoin the Union. Also,

> What was the purpose of Reconstruction?
>
> _____
>
> _____

only southerners who swore they had never
supported the Confederacy could run for office.
Lincoln refused to sign the bill.

FREEDOM FOR AFRICAN AMERICANS

In 1865 the **Thirteenth Amendment** to the
Constitution officially outlawed slavery in the
nation. Former slaves reacted to freedom in many
ways. They legalized their marriages, searched for
relatives who had been sold, took new last names,
and moved to new places.

> **What part of the Constitution granted freedom to all slaves?**
>
> _____
>
> _____

   To help the South's poor and freedpeople,
Congress created the **Freedmen's Bureau** in 1865.
One of its roles was to build more schools. Some
freedpeople also established their own schools.
Although some southerners violently resisted the
idea of educating African Americans,
freedpeople of all ages attended classes.

> **Why would southerners oppose the education of African Americans?**
>
> _____
>
> _____
>
> _____

PRESIDENT JOHNSON'S RECONSTRUCTION PLAN

On April 14, 1865, President Lincoln was shot
while attending the theater. He died the next
morning. Vice-President **Andrew Johnson** became
the next president. Johnson's Reconstruction plan
included a way to restructure southern state
governments. States that followed the steps were
to be readmitted to the Union.

> **Why did Congress refuse to accept the southern states back into the Union?**
>
> _____
>
> _____
>
> _____

   Most of the southern states followed Johnson's
plan, but Congress refused to accept them back
into the Union. Many of the elected
representatives of the "new" states had been
Confederate leaders. Clearly there were still
problems to be solved.

CHALLENGE ACTIVITY

Critical Thinking: Explain You are a citizen from
a southern state. Write a letter to Congress
explaining why it is your right to choose your
state's representatives.

| Andrew Johnson | Reconstruction | Thirteenth Amendment |
| Freedmen's Bureau | Ten Percent Plan | |

DIRECTIONS Read each sentence and choose the correct term from the word bank to replace the underlined phrase. Write the term in the space provided and then define the term in your own words.

1. The time of reuniting the nation and rebuilding the southern states without slavery was called <u>Ten Percent Plan</u>. _____

   Your definition: _____
   _____

2. The <u>Thirteenth Amendment</u> was established to provide relief for poor people, black and white, in the South. _____

   Your definition: _____
   _____

3. The <u>Freedmen's Bureau</u> was the vice-president sworn into office after President Lincoln was shot while attending the theater and later died.
   _____

   Your definition: _____
   _____

4. Lincoln offered southerners amnesty for all illegal acts supporting the rebellion under the <u>Thirteenth Amendment</u>. _____

   Your definition: _____
   _____

5. Slavery was made illegal throughout the United States under the <u>Ten Percent Plan</u>. _____

   Your definition: _____
   _____

Reconstruction

MAIN IDEAS
1. Black Codes led to opposition to President Johnson's plan for Reconstruction.
2. The Fourteenth Amendment ensured citizenship for African Americans.
3. Radical Republicans in Congress took charge of Reconstruction.
4. The Fifteenth Amendment gave African Americans the right to vote.

Key Terms and People

Black Codes southern laws that greatly limited the freedom of African Americans

Radical Republicans Republicans who wanted more federal control in Reconstruction

Civil Rights Act of 1866 act giving African Americans the same legal rights as whites

Fourteenth Amendment amendment guaranteeing citizens equal protection of laws

Reconstruction Acts laws passed to protect African American rights

impeachment process of bringing charges of wrongdoing against a public official

Fifteenth Amendment amendment giving African American men the right to vote

Lesson Summary
OPPOSITION TO PRESIDENT JOHNSON

Almost as soon as the southern states created new legislatures, those legislatures went to work passing **Black Codes**. The Black Codes were laws that greatly limited the freedom of African Americans. In fact, the codes created working conditions that resembled slavery for African Americans. Many African Americans organized to protest codes.

The Black Codes angered many Republicans who believed the South was returning to its old ways. The **Radical Republicans** wanted the federal government to step in. They wanted more federal

What were Black Codes?

_____

_____

_____

Who believed President Johnson's Reconstruction plan was a failure?

_____

_____

Guided Reading Workbook

Lesson 2, *continued*

control over Reconstruction to make sure southern leaders did not remain loyal to the old Confederate principles. One Radical Republican leader was Pennsylvania's Thaddeus Stevens. Stevens and others pushed for racial equality. They branded Johnson's Reconstruction plan a failure.

FOURTEENTH AMENDMENT

In 1866 Congress proposed a bill to give more power to the Freedmen's Bureau. President Johnson vetoed it. He believed Congress could not pass new laws until the South was represented in Congress.

> **Circle the verb that shows that President Johnson was against the Civil Rights Act of 1866.**

Then Congress proposed the **Civil Rights Act of 1866**. It guaranteed African Americans the same legal rights as whites. Johnson vetoed this, too. Congress overrode the veto. It also proposed the Fourteenth Amendment to secure these protections.

CONGRESS TAKES CONTROL OF RECONSTRUCTION

After the 1866 elections, Republicans held a two-thirds majority in both the House and Senate. As a result, Congress passed several **Reconstruction Acts**. It also passed a law limiting the president's powers to remove cabinet members without Senate approval. When President Johnson broke that law by firing his secretary of war, Congress reacted by impeaching the president. The **impeachment** fell short by one vote. Johnson remained president, though he had little authority or influence.

> **Why was President Johnson impeached?**
> _____
> _____

FIFTEENTH AMENDMENT

Republicans believed that African Americans would support the Reconstruction plan. To gain their votes, Republicans in Congress proposed the **Fifteenth Amendment**, which guaranteed

> **Which Americans gained the right to vote as a result of the Fifteenth Amendment?**
> _____
> _____

Guided Reading Workbook

African American men the right to vote. This
amendment went into effect in 1870.

CHALLENGE ACTIVITY

Critical Thinking: Summarize Find the
Constitution in your textbook and read the entire
Fourteenth and Fifteenth Amendments. Write a
sentence summarizing each amendment.

DIRECTIONS On the line provided before each statement, write **T** if
a statement is true and **F** if a statement is false. If the statement is
false, write the correct term on the line after each sentence that
makes the sentence a true statement.

_____ 1. The Civil Rights Act of 1866 provided African Americans with the
same legal rights as white Americans.

_____

_____ 2. The Fifteenth Amendment gave all African American men throughout
the United States the right to vote.

_____

_____ 3. The Reconstruction Acts were laws that restricted the overall freedom
of African Americans.

_____

_____ 4. Thaddeus Stevens was a leader of the Radical Republicans, who
wanted racial equality for all Americans, including newly freed ones.

_____

_____ 5. The Black Codes were laws passed by the Republican-controlled
Congress to protect the rights of African Americans.

_____

_____ 6. The Radical Republicans wanted the South to change much more than
it already had before returning to the Union.

_____

_____ 7. The Fourteenth Amendment ensured citizenship for African
Americans.

_____

Reconstruction

MAIN IDEAS
1. Reconstruction governments helped reform the South.
2. The Ku Klux Klan was organized as African Americans moved into positions of power.
3. As Reconstruction ended, the rights of African Americans were restricted.
4. Southern business leaders relied on industry to rebuild the South.

Key Terms and People

Hiram Revels first African American senator

Ku Klux Klan secret society that used violence to oppress African Americans

Enforcement Acts laws providing equal protection for all under the law

Compromise of 1877 agreement in which Democrats accepted Hayes's election to the presidency in exchange for removing federal troops from the South

poll tax special tax people had to pay before they could vote

segregation forced separation of whites and African Americans in public places

Jim Crow laws laws that enforced segregation

Plessy* v. *Ferguson Supreme Court ruling that upheld segregation

sharecropping system in which farm laborers kept, or shared, some of the crop

Lesson Summary
RECONSTRUCTION GOVERNMENTS
Southerners did not trust northern Republicans who had moved south. They thought the newcomers sought profit from Reconstruction. African Americans used their new right to vote to elect more than 600 African Americans. The first black senator was **Hiram Revels**.

> Who was the first African American senator?
> _____

KU KLUX KLAN
In 1866 a group of southerners created the secret and violent **Ku Klux Klan**. Its targets were African Americans, Republicans, and public officials. The Klan spread throughout the South until the federal government passed the

> Circle the groups of Americans that were targeted by the Ku Klux Klan.

Enforcement Acts. The **Enforcement Acts** made Klan activities illegal.

RECONSTRUCTION ENDS

The General Amnesty Act of 1872 allowed most former Confederates to serve in public office. Soon many Democratic ex-Confederates were elected. Republicans also lost power because of Grant's problem-plagued presidency and the Panic of 1873. In 1876 the Hayes-Tilden presidential race was so close, it took the **Compromise of 1877** to make sure Democrats would accept Hayes's election.

Southern Democrats, called Redeemers, worked to limit African American rights. The methods they used included **poll taxes**, legal **segregation**, and **Jim Crow laws**. They even got help from the Supreme Court, which ruled in *Plessy v. Ferguson* that segregation was legal.

African Americans found their rights restricted in other ways, too. Most African Americans could not afford to buy land, so many began **sharecropping**. Sharecropping is sharing a crop with landowners. Often only the landowner profited. Sharecroppers lived in debt.

> **Why did southern Republicans lose power during the 1870s?**
>
> _____
>
> _____
>
> _____

REBUILDING SOUTHERN INDUSTRY

The South's economy depended on cotton profits, which went up and down. In the "New South" movement, southern leaders turned to industry to strengthen the economy. Mills and factories were built. The new industries thrived and helped the southern economy grow stronger.

> **How was the economy of the "Old South" different from the economy of the "New South"?**
>
> _____
>
> _____
>
> _____

RECONSTRUCTION IN THE NORTH

The new right of African American men to vote inspired women to work for their own suffrage. Northern African Americans gained some additional freedoms as well.

CHALLENGE ACTIVITY

Critical Thinking: Explain Write a paragraph
explaining how the General Amnesty Act
eventually led to the Compromise of 1877.

DIRECTIONS Read each sentence and fill in the blank with the
word in the word pair that best completes the sentence.

1. A special tax that people had to pay before they could vote was called
   _____. (a poll tax/Jim Crow laws)

2. _____ was a system in which the landowners provided
   the land, tools, and supplies and workers provided the labor. (Segregation/
   Sharecropping)

3. In _____, the U.S. Supreme Court allowed segregation
   if "separate-but-equal" facilities were provided. (the Compromise of 1877/
   Plessy v. *Ferguson*)

4. _____ was the first African American in the U.S.
   Senate. (Hiram Revels/James Alcorn)

5. The removal of remaining troops from the South, funding for internal
   improvements, and the appointment of a southern Democrat to the
   president's cabinet were part of the _____. (Jim Crow
   laws/Compromise of 1877)

6. The forced separation of whites and African Americans in public places is
   called _____. (segregation/Ku Klux Klan)

7. The _____ was a secret society that opposed civil
   rights for African Americans and used violence and terror against them. (Ku
   Klux Klan/Jim Crow laws)

8. _____ were approved in southern states in the 1880s
   and allowed southerners to legally discriminate against African Americans.
   (Jim Crow laws/Segregationists)

Westward Expansion

MAIN IDEAS

1. As American settlers moved west, control of the Mississippi River became more important to the United States.
2. Expeditions led by Lewis, Clark, and Frémont increased Americans' understanding of the West.
3. During the early 1800s, Americans moved west of the Rocky Mountains to settle and trade.
4. Families moved into the far west and established thriving communities.

Key Terms and People

Daniel Boone guide who was first to lead settlers beyond the Appalachians; cut a road west

Louisiana Purchase the purchase of Louisiana from France for $15 million, which roughly doubled the size of the United States

Meriwether Lewis a former army captain chosen by President Thomas Jefferson to lead an expedition to explore the West

William Clark co-leader of the western expedition

Lewis and Clark expedition a long journey to explore the Louisiana Purchase

Sacagawea a Shoshone who helped the Lewis and Clark expedition by naming plants and gathering edible fruits and vegetables for the group

Zebulon Pike an explorer of the West who reached the summit of the mountain now known as Pike's Peak

John C. Frémont led an expedition to the Rocky Mountains in 1842 and wrote a report of his journey that became a guide for future travelers to the West

mountain men fur traders and trappers who traveled to the Rocky Mountains and the Pacific Northwest in the early 1800s

John Jacob Astor owner of the American Fur Company who founded the first important settlement in Oregon Country in 1811

Oregon Trail the main route from the Mississippi River to the West Coast in the early 1800s

Santa Fe Trail the route from Independence, Missouri, to Santa Fe, New Mexico

Mormons members of a religious group, formally known as the Church of Jesus Christ of Latter-day Saints, who moved west during the 1830s and 1840s

Brigham Young Mormon leader who chose Utah as the group's new home

Lesson Summary

THE FIRST WESTERNERS

In 1775 **Daniel Boone** led a group that cut a road west through the Cumberland Gap in Kentucky. Thousands of Americans moved to the area between the Appalachians and the Mississippi River. The setters used the Mississippi and Ohio rivers to move products east. New Orleans was an essential port for river trade. Spain governed New Orleans.

> **Why was the Mississippi River important?**
> _____
> _____

LOUISIANA AND WESTERN EXPLORERS

In 1802 Spain shut American shipping out of New Orleans. Then they traded Louisiana to France. President Thomas Jefferson sent ambassadors to France. When the ambassadors tried to buy New Orleans, France offered to sell the entire territory of Louisiana. The United States bought the western territory for $15 million in the **Louisiana Purchase**.

> **Why did Jefferson send ambassadors to France?**
> _____
> _____

President Jefferson wanted to learn more about the West and the Native Americans who lived there. He also wondered if there was a river route to the Pacific Ocean.

> **Underline the sentences that explain what Jefferson wanted to learn about the West.**

In 1803 Congress provided money to explore the West. **Meriwether Lewis** and **William Clark** were chosen to lead the **Lewis and Clark expedition**, which began in May 1804.

Lewis and Clark and their crew traveled up the Missouri River. They saw Native Americans, and Lewis used interpreters to tell their leaders that the United States now owned the land on which they lived. **Sacagawea** (sak-uh-guh-WEE-uh) and her husband aided Lewis and Clark. Lewis and Clark did not find a river route to the Pacific, but they learned much about western lands.

> **What message did Lewis and Clark give to Native Americans?**
> _____
> _____
> _____

In 1806 **Zebulon Pike** was sent to locate the Red River. The Red River was the Louisiana Territory's border with New Spain. In present-day Colorado he reached the summit of Pike's

Peak. Pike gave many Americans their first information about the Southwest.

Another explorer, **John C. Frémont**, led an expedition to the Rocky Mountains in 1842. He wrote a report of his journey that became a guide for future travelers. The information he gave made many more settlers eager to move west.

MOUNTAIN MEN GO WEST

In the early 1800s trappers and traders known as **mountain men** worked to supply the eastern fashion for fur hats and clothing. **John Jacob Astor**, owner of the American Fur Company, sent mountain men to the Pacific Northwest region that became known as Oregon Country.

TRAILS WEST

Many Americans began to move to Oregon Country. Most of them followed a route that became known as the **Oregon Trail**. It was common for families to band together and undertake the perilous six-month journey in wagon trains.

Mainly traders used another well-traveled route west, the **Santa Fe Trail**. They loaded wagon trains with cloth and other manufactured goods. They traded the goods for horses, mules, and silver in the Mexican settlement of Santa Fe.

One large group of settlers traveled to the West in search of religious freedom. They were known as **Mormons**, members of the Church of Jesus Christ of Latter-day Saints. Thousands of Mormons took the Mormon Trail. They traveled to an area near the Great Salt Lake in what is now Utah. **Brigham Young**, their leader, chose that site. By 1860 there were about 40,000 Mormons living in Utah.

> What was the result of John C. Frémont's report on his journey west?
> _____
> _____
> _____

> Circle the names of three trails people used traveling west.

> What group traveled west in search of religious freedom?
> _____

CHALLENGE ACTIVITY

Critical Thinking: Draw Inferences Some members of the Lewis and Clark expedition kept journals or diaries. Write a brief diary entry as if you were a member of the expedition.

DIRECTIONS Match the terms in the first list with their correct definitions from the second list by placing the letter of the correct definition in the space provided before each term.

_____ 1. John Jacob Astor

_____ 2. Brigham Young

_____ 3. Daniel Boone

_____ 4. Santa Fe Trail

_____ 5. Zebulon Pike

_____ 6. Louisiana Purchase

_____ 7. Lewis and Clark expedition

_____ 8. Oregon Trail

_____ 9. Sacagawea

_____ 10. John C. Frémont

a. led an expedition to the Rocky Mountains in 1842 and wrote a report of his journey that became a guide for future travelers to the West

b. payment to France of $15 million, which roughly doubled the size of the United States

c. the route from Independence, Missouri, to Santa Fe, New Mexico

d. guide who was first to lead settlers beyond the Appalachians; cut a road west

e. Mormon leader who chose Utah as the group's new home

f. owner of the American Fur Company who founded the first important settlement in Oregon Country in 1811

g. Shoshone woman who helped the Lewis and Clark expedition by gathering edible fruits and vegetables for the group

h. the main route from the Mississippi River to the West Coast in the early 1800s

i. a long journey to explore the Louisiana Purchase

j. an explorer of the West who reached the summit of the mountain now known as Pike's Peak

Westward Expansion

MAIN IDEAS
1. Valuable deposits of gold and silver in the West created opportunities for wealth and brought more settlers to the region.
2. The cattle industry thrived on the Great Plains, supplying beef to the East.
3. The transcontinental railroad succeeded in linking the eastern and western United States.

Key Terms and People

frontier an area that is undeveloped

Comstock Lode name given to 1859 gold and silver discovery in western Nevada

boomtowns towns that serviced new mines and emptied when the mines closed

Cattle Kingdom the name given to the Great Plains during the years when they supported great herds of cattle

cattle drive movement of cattle herds to market or new grazing lands

Chisholm Trail a popular route for cattle drives from San Antonio to Abilene, Kansas

Pony Express mail delivery system in which messengers transported mail on horseback across the country

transcontinental railroad railroad across United States, connecting East and West

standard time system developed by railroad companies dividing the United States into four time zones

Lesson Summary

MINING BOOM BRINGS GROWTH

Around the time of the Civil War, most Americans thought of the Great Plains as the Great American Desert. After the Civil War, many Americans moved west. By 1850 the **frontier**, or undeveloped region, had reached the Pacific Ocean.

Settlers built homes and fenced off land. They started ranches and farms. Miners, ranchers, and farmers adapted to their new surroundings.

> How would the environment in the frontier change as a result of the settlers?
>
> _____
>
> _____
>
> _____

In 1859 miners found gold and silver in western Nevada. News of the **Comstock Lode** (named after miner Henry Comstock) brought thousands to Nevada. Most miners could not afford the expensive equipment needed to remove gold and silver from quartz. They sold their claims to big businesses. Mining jobs were dangerous and low paying. Many immigrants came to work in the mines. As mines opened, **boomtowns** appeared. These were communities that grew suddenly. When the mines closed down, most boomtowns did too.

> How did the discovery of precious metals affect Nevada's population?
>
> _____
>
> _____

THE CATTLE KINGDOM

Demand for beef in the East led to a booming cattle industry in Texas. Soon the cattle industry spread onto the Great Plains, creating a huge **Cattle Kingdom** with giant herds grazing the open range.

Cowboys cared for the cattle. They were responsible for the long **cattle drives** that got the cattle to Abilene, Kansas. There, the new railroad could ship the cattle to markets far away. The **Chisholm Trail** was one of these routes.

> Underline the sentence that helps you to infer that cattle need large parcels of land for grazing.

THE TRANSCONTINENTAL RAILROAD

In 1860 the **Pony Express** improved communication between the East and the West. But it was replaced in 1861 by the telegraph, which could send messages much faster.

By 1862 Congress started passing laws that supported the building of a **transcontinental railroad**. By the end of 1863, the work had begun. One railroad line was building from the East and one from the West. In 1889 the two lines met at Promontory, Utah. Soon, railroads crisscrossed the country.

Railroads provided better transportation for people and goods all over America. Rail travel also connected people in new ways. Before the

> Based on what you have read, how would you define the word *transcontinental*?
>
> _____
>
> _____
>
> _____

Guided Reading Workbook

railroads, each community determined its own
time based on the sun. This caused problems for
people who scheduled trains crossing a long
distance. Railroad companies established
standard time, dividing the United States into
four time zones. By 1890 railroads were one of
the nation's biggest industries.

CHALLENGE ACTIVITY

Critical Thinking: Evaluate Research the Pony
Express to find out why it operated for only 18
months. Write an essay giving your opinion about
whether the Pony Express was a success.

DIRECTIONS Look at each set of three vocabulary
terms. On the line provided, write the letter of the term
that does not relate to the others.

_____ 1. a. Cattle Kingdom
        b. cattle drive
        c. Pony Express

_____ 2. a. Comstock Lode
        b. Chisholm Trail
        c. cattle drive

_____ 3. a. boomtowns
        b. frontier
        c. Comstock Lode

_____ 4. a. cowboys
        b. cattle drive
        c. boomtowns

_____ 5. a. Pony Express
        b. transcontinental railroad
        c. standard time

_____ 6. a. transcontinental railroad
        b. Pony Express
        c. cowboys

_____ 7. a. cattle drive
        b. Comstock Lode
        c. open range

DIRECTIONS Read each sentence and fill in the blank with the word
in the word pair that best completes the sentence.

8. Producing over $500 million worth of gold and silver, the

_____ was a bonanza—a large deposit of

precious ore. (Comstock Lode/frontier)

9. Often lasting several months and covering hundreds of miles, a _____ was one of a cowboy's most important and dangerous duties. (open range/cattle drive)

10. Congress passed laws that supported the building of the _____. (Pony Express/transcontinental railroad)

Westward Expansion

Lesson 3

MAIN IDEAS
1. As settlers moved to the Great Plains, they encountered the Plains Indians.
2. Native Americans attempted to keep their lands through treaties with the U.S. government.
3. Continued pressure from white settlement and government legislation brought the Plains Indians' traditional way of life to an end.

Key Terms and People

Treaty of Fort Laramie first major agreement signed with northern Plains nations

reservations areas of federal land set aside for Native Americans

Crazy Horse Sioux leader who violently protested reservations

Treaty of Medicine Lodge southern Plains Indians agreed to live on reservations

buffalo soldiers nickname given by Indians to African American cavalry

Sitting Bull Sioux leader who defeated Custer at Little Bighorn

George Armstrong Custer army commander who lost to the Sioux at Little Bighorn

Battle of the Little Bighorn last great victory for Sioux, where they defeated Custer

Massacre at Wounded Knee battle in which U.S. troops killed about 150 Sioux

Long Walk a 300-mile forced march of Navajo captives to a reservation

Chief Joseph Nez Percé chief who fled to Canada before being forced to a reservation

Geronimo Apache leader who continued to fight against the U.S. Army until 1886

Ghost Dance religious movement predicting a paradise for Native Americans

Sarah Winnemucca Paiute against the government's treatment of Native Americans

assimilate give up traditional ways and adopt the ways of a different group

Dawes General Allotment Act act that took almost 70 percent of reservation land

Lesson Summary

SETTLERS ENCOUNTER THE PLAINS INDIANS

As miners and settlers began crossing the Great Plains in the mid-1800s, they wanted access to more lands. The U.S. government tried to avoid disputes by negotiating the **Treaty of Fort Laramie**. It was the first major treaty between the U.S. government and the northern Plains Indians. Other treaties created **reservations** for Indians. Many refused to move. In 1866 **Crazy Horse** and his Sioux warriors killed 81 soldiers. By the 1867 **Treaty of Medicine Lodge**, most southern Plains Indians agreed to go to reservations.

> **What did settlers want that Indians had?**
> _____
> _____

> **Why do you think that many Native Americans fought the move to reservations?**
> _____
> _____
> _____

FIGHTING ON THE PLAINS

Native Americans of the northern Plains, Southwest, and Far West continued to resist reservations. The U.S. government sent **buffalo soldiers** and other troops to force Indians to leave.

In 1874 gold was discovered in the Black Hills of the Dakotas. The government wanted the Sioux to sell their reservation. **Sitting Bull** and other Sioux refused. In response, Lieutenant Colonel **George Armstrong Custer** ordered his soldiers to attack the Sioux. The Sioux won what became known as the **Battle of the Little Bighorn**. In the last great battle of the Plains Indians, 150 Sioux men, women, and children were killed in the **Massacre at Wounded Knee**.

Other Native Americans also fought forced removal. The Navajo tried to resist, but facing starvation, surrendered. They were led on a forced march to a reservation that became known as the **Long Walk**. Many died along the way.

Resistance also came from **Chief Joseph** and a group of Nez Percé, who wanted to keep their land in Oregon. In 1877 they fled across the border to Canada, but were captured by U.S.

> **Why did the government want the Sioux to sell their reservation?**
> _____
> _____
> _____

> **How did Chief Joseph and the group he led resist relocating to a reservation?**
> _____
> _____

troops and sent to a reservation. In 1886 Apache leader **Geronimo** and his warrior band surrendered, which ended Apache armed resistance.

A WAY OF LIFE ENDS

By the 1870s many Native Americans lived on reservations where land was not useful for farming or buffalo hunting. Many were starving. A Paiute leader named Wovoka started a religious movement, the **Ghost Dance**. It predicted paradise for Indians. But officials feared this movement would lead to rebellion. **Sarah Winnemucca**, another Paiute, called for reform of the reservation system.

Some reformers believed that Native Americans should **assimilate** by adopting the ways of white people. The **Dawes General Allotment Act** of 1887 took about two-thirds of Indian reservation land.

> **Why did officials worry about the spread of the Ghost Dance beliefs?**
>
> _____
>
> _____

CHALLENGE ACTIVITY

Critical Thinking: Evaluate Choose a group of people: pioneers, miners, Sioux, soldiers. Write a paragraph describing how you think that group of people reacted to Custer's defeat.

Ghost Dance	Dawes General Allotment Act	reservations
buffalo soldiers	Battle of the Little Bighorn	Sarah Winnemucca
Chief Joseph	Long Walk	Sitting Bull
Crazy Horse	Massacre at Wounded Knee	Treaty of Fort Laramie

DIRECTIONS Read each sentence and chose a term from the word bank to fill in the blank.

1. _____ was a Sioux leader who defeated Custer at Little Bighorn.

2. The first major agreement signed with northern Plains nations was the _____.

3. _____ are areas of federal land set aside for Native Americans.

4. The nickname given by Indians to African American cavalry was _____.

5. The Navajos called a 300-mile forced march to a reservation the _____.

6. _____ called for reform of the reservation system.

7. The act that took back two-thirds of Indian land was the _____.

8. In the _____, the last great battle of the Plains Indians, 150 Sioux men, women, and children were killed.

9. A Paiute leader named Wovoka started a religious movement, the _____, that officials feared would lead to rebellion.

10. _____ and a group of Nez Percé wanted to keep their land in Oregon. They fled across the border to Canada before being forced to a reservation.

Guided Reading Workbook

> **MAIN IDEAS**
> 1. Many Americans started new lives on the Great Plains.
> 2. Economic challenges led to the creation of farmers' political groups.
> 3. By the 1890s the western frontier had come to an end.

Key Terms and People

Homestead Act an 1862 act that gave government-owned land to farmers

Morrill Act an 1862 act that gave government-owned land to the states, with the understanding that the states would sell the land to finance colleges

Exodusters African Americans who left the South for Kansas in 1879

sodbusters nickname given to Great Plains farmers because breaking the soil was such hard work

dry farming farming using hardy crops that need less water than others

Annie Bidwell a Great Plains pioneer-reformer

deflation a decrease in the money supply and overall lower prices

National Grange a social and educational organization for farmers

William Jennings Bryan Democratic candidate for president in the 1888 election

Populist Party new national party formed by the country's farmers

Lesson Summary
NEW LIVES ON THE PLAINS

In 1862 two acts helped open the West to settlers. The **Homestead Act** gave government-owned land to small farmers. The **Morrill Act** granted millions of acres of government land to the states. The states would then sell that land and use the money to build colleges.

These acts attracted many groups to the Great Plains. This included single women who could get land through the Homestead Act. It also included up to 40,000 African Americans. Some called them **Exodusters** because of their exodus from the South. **Sodbusters** earned their nickname because breaking up the sod of the Great Plains was hard work. **Dry farming** helped

> Underline the two congressional acts in 1862 that helped settle the West.

> How did sodbusters get their nickname?
> _____
> _____
> _____

Lesson 4, *continued*

the sodbusters succeed. In addition, the steel plow developed by John Deere, the windmill, barbed wire, and mechanical reapers and threshers all made farmwork more efficient.

Circle the inventions that made farming the Plains more efficient.

Some pioneer women, such as author Laura Ingalls Wilder and suffragist **Annie Bidwell**, became famous. Most settlers lived a lonely life, though. They were isolated on the remote farms of the Plains. Early farmers also had to build their own communities.

FARMERS' POLITICAL GROUPS

Modern machines made farming more productive. This productivity, however, led to overproduction, which in turn led to lower crop prices. To make matters worse, at this time the U.S. economy was affected by **deflation**, in which the money supply decreased and prices dropped. So although farmers farmed more, they made less money for their crops. Many lost their farms during this time.

Why could banding together help farmers? _____ _____ _____

To help each other, farmers formed the **National Grange** (*grange* is an old word for "granary"). The Grange worked to better farmers' lives. It worked to get the railroads regulated. It also backed political candidates such as **William Jennings Bryan**.

In 1892 political organizations called Farmers' Alliances formed a new pro-farmer political party. They called it the **Populist Party**. In the 1896 presidential elections, it supported Democrat Bryan. Bryan lost and the Populist Party dissolved.

Why do you think the Populist Party dissolved after Bryan lost the presidential election? _____ _____ _____

END OF THE FRONTIER

In 1889 the government opened Oklahoma to homesteaders. These pioneers quickly claimed more than 11 million acres of land. The frontier existed no more.

What ended America's frontier? _____ _____ _____

Guided Reading Workbook

CHALLENGE ACTIVITY

Critical Thinking: Analyze Tell why
overproduction on farms could lead to lower
prices for crops.

DIRECTIONS Read each sentence and fill in the
blank with the word in the word pair that best
completes the sentence.

1. _____ emphasized the planting of hardy crops that need
   less water than other crops. (Exodusters/Dry farming)

2. _____ was a political candidate for the Populist Party.
   (William Jennings Bryan/John Deere)

3. The states were granted millions of acres of federal land through the
   _____. (Morrill Act/National Grange)

4. The _____ was a social and educational organization
   that sought to improve the quality of life for farmers and their families.
   (Morrill Act/National Grange)

5. _____ earned their nickname because of the hard work
   needed to break up the sod of the Great Plains. (Sodbusters/Exodusters)

6. _____ was a well-known pioneer woman who supported
   a number of moral and social causes, including the women's suffrage
   movement. (Laura Ingalls Wilder/Annie Bidwell)

7. Political organizations called Farmers' Alliances formed the new national
   pro-farmer _____. (Populist Party/Sodbusters)

8. Through the _____, passed by Congress in 1862,
   individual citizens could receive land. (Homestead Act/Morrill Act)

9. _____ were those African Americans who left the South
   in the late nineteenth century, seeking land in Kansas being offered by the
   federal government under the Homestead Act. (Exodusters/National Grange)

The Industrial Age

MAIN IDEAS
1. Breakthroughs in steel processing led to a boom in railroad construction.
2. Advances in the use of oil and electricity improved communications and transportation.
3. A rush of inventions changed Americans' lives.

Key Terms and People

Second Industrial Revolution a period of rapid growth in U.S. manufacturing in the late 1800s; characterized by advances in technology

Bessemer process Henry Bessemer's invention that was a way to manufacture steel quickly and cheaply

Thomas Edison inventor who created the electric lightbulb

Alexander Graham Bell inventor of the telephone

patent an exclusive right to make or sell an invention; encouraged new inventions

Henry Ford inventor of the first affordable car and the moving assembly line

Wilbur and Orville Wright brothers who made the first piloted flight in a gas-powered airplane

Lesson Summary
BREAKTHROUGHS IN STEEL PROCESSING

America's **Second Industrial Revolution** started in the late 1800s. The new **Bessemer process** reduced the amount of time it took to make steel. The price of steel dropped, increasing steel production. This made the steel industry important to the revolution.

Cheaper, more available steel led to more railroad building. Other changes made train travel safer and smoother for passengers. Trains helped strengthen the economy by moving people and goods to their destinations quickly and inexpensively.

> What effect did inexpensive, readily available steel have on the railroad industry?
>
> _____
>
> _____
>
> _____

USE OF OIL AND ELECTRICITY

In the 1850s scientists figured out how to turn crude oil into kerosene. Kerosene was used for both heat and light. As a result, the demand for oil exploded. In 1859 Edwin L. Drake's Titusville, Pennsylvania, oil well started producing 20 barrels of oil a day. Oil quickly became big business in Pennsylvania. Oil was also important in Ohio and West Virginia.

In addition to oil, electricity became a source of light and power. **Thomas Edison** was an inventor interested in uses of electricity. In 1879 Edison and his assistants created the electric lightbulb. To create a market for his product, Edison built a power plant to supply industries with electricity. George Westinghouse developed a power system that could send electricity over long distances. Thanks to Edison and Westinghouse the use of electricity in homes and businesses boomed.

> **What made the demand for oil rise in the 1850s?**
> _____
> _____

> **How did Edison and Westinghouse help spread the use of electricity?**
> _____
> _____

RUSH OF INVENTIONS

Technology also changed the way people communicated. First, telegraphs made long-distance communication possible. However, the telegraph dealt with only written messages. In 1876 **Alexander Graham Bell** made it possible for people to communicate by speech over long distances. He was given a **patent** for the telephone. By 1900 almost 1.5 million telephones were in operation.

Changes in transportation also occurred. The invention of the gasoline-powered engine made automobiles possible. **Henry Ford** began producing the first affordable automobile, the Model T, in 1908. He also implemented the moving assembly line in manufacturing. The gas-powered engine allowed **Wilbur and Orville Wright** to invent the airplane.

> **What invention made automobiles possible?**
> _____
> _____

CHALLENGE ACTIVITY

Critical Thinking: Make Judgments Review all of
the inventions about which you just read. In your
opinion, which was the most life changing? Why?

Alexander Graham Bell	Orville and Wilbur Wright	telephone
Bessemer process	patent	
Henry Ford	Second Industrial Revolution	

DIRECTIONS Write two descriptive phrases that describe each
person or term.

1. Alexander Graham Bell _____

_____

2. Bessemer process _____

_____

3. Orville and Wilbur Wright _____

_____

4. patent _____

_____

5. Second Industrial Revolution _____

_____

6. Thomas Alva Edison _____

_____

7. Henry Ford _____

_____

DIRECTIONS Answer each question by writing a sentence that contains at least one word from the word bank.

8. The development of what new technique dramatically reduced the amount of time needed to process iron ore into steel?

_____

_____

9. Which inventor, and which invention, allowed people to communicate over long distances by talking?

_____

_____

10. Name the period of rapid growth in U.S. manufacturing at the end of the 1800s.

_____

_____

The Industrial Age

MAIN IDEAS
1. The rise of corporations and powerful business leaders led to the dominance of big businesses in the United States.
2. People and the government began to question the methods of big business.

Key Terms and People

corporations businesses that sell portions of ownership called stock shares

Andrew Carnegie business leader who concentrated his efforts on steel production

vertical integration ownership of businesses involved in each step of manufacturing

John D. Rockefeller business leader who concentrated on oil refining

horizontal integration owning all businesses in a certain field

trust a legal arrangement grouping together a number of companies under a single board of directors

Leland Stanford business leader of mining equipment and railroads

social Darwinism belief that Charles Darwin's theory of natural selection and "survival of the fittest" holds true for humans

monopoly total ownership of a product or service

Sherman Antitrust Act law passed in 1890 that made it illegal to create monopolies or trusts that restrained trade

Lesson Summary
DOMINANCE OF BIG BUSINESS

In the late 1800s entrepreneurs began to form **corporations**. A corporation is owned by people who buy shares of stock in that corporation. Stockholders share the corporation's profits. But if the corporation fails, stockholders lose the money that they invested. Entrepreneurs could spread the risk of loss across all the stockholders.

One successful entrepreneur of the late 1800s was **Andrew Carnegie**. He made money in several industries, but he focused on steel. Carnegie bought out his competitors when steel prices

> **Why did entrepreneurs form corporations in the late 1800s?**
>
> _____
>
> _____
>
> _____

were low. In doing so, he acquired all the
businesses involved in making steel. This is called
vertical integration.

John D. Rockefeller made his fortune in oil.
Like Carnegie, he used vertical integration. By
1880 he also owned 90 percent of the oil-refining
business in the United States, which is **horizontal
integration**. He grouped his companies into a
trust to control oil production and prices.

Leland Stanford was another successful
business leader. He made money selling mining
equipment to miners. He also helped found the
Central Pacific Railroad.

> **What did Andrew Carnegie,
> John D. Rockefeller, and
> Leland Stanford have in
> common?**
>
> _____
>
> _____

QUESTIONING THE METHODS OF BIG BUSINESS

In the late 1800s many business leaders believed
in **social Darwinism**. Charles Darwin proposed
that in nature, the law was "survival of the
fittest." Social Darwinists believed the same was
true of humans—those who got rich were the
fittest.

> **What is social Darwinism?**
>
> _____
>
> _____
>
> _____

Other wealthy business leaders claimed that the
rich had a duty to help the poor. As a result,
some leaders gave millions of dollars to charities.

Big business caused problems for smaller ones.
A big business would lower its prices until small
businesses, unable to offer the same low prices,
went bankrupt. Consumers then had to pay
higher prices because there was no longer any
competition.

Americans demanded that Congress pass laws
to control **monopolies** and trusts. Congress finally
passed the **Sherman Antitrust Act**. However, the
act did little to reduce the power of corporations.

> **Why did some people think
> monopolies and trusts
> were bad for society?**
>
> _____
>
> _____
>
> _____

CHALLENGE ACTIVITY

Critical Thinking: Evaluate You are an adviser to
the president. Voters are complaining about big
discount stores putting small, family-owned
stores out of business by lowering prices. Make a

list of advantages and disadvantages of large
stores. Write a summary of your list and advise
the president.

DIRECTIONS On the line provided before each statement, write **T** if
a statement is true and **F** if a statement is false. If the statement is
false, write the correct term on the line after each sentence that
makes the sentence a true statement.

_____ 1. A trust is a legal arrangement grouping together a number of
companies under a single board of directors.

_____

_____ 2. Passed by Congress in 1890, the Sherman Antitrust Act was largely
ineffective because it did little to reduce the power of corporations.

_____

_____ 3. Corporations are businesses that sell portions of ownership called
stock shares.

_____

_____ 4. Owning the businesses involved in each step of a manufacturing
process is called horizontal integration.

_____

_____ 5. John D. Rockefeller became successful through combining, or
consolidating, businesses.

_____

_____ 6. Rockefeller's ownership of 90 percent of the oil-refining business in the
United States by 1880 is an example of vertical integration.

_____

_____ 7. Andrew Carnegie focused his efforts on steelmaking and expanded his
business by buying out his competitors when steel prices were low.

_____

The Industrial Age

MAIN IDEAS
1. The desire to maximize profits and become more efficient led to poor working conditions.
2. Workers began to organize and demand improvements in working conditions and pay.
3. Labor strikes often turned violent and failed to accomplish their goals.

Key Terms and People

Frederick W. Taylor author of *The Principles of Scientific Management*

Knights of Labor large labor union that included both skilled and unskilled workers

Terence V. Powderly Knights of Labor leader who made it the first national labor union in the United States

American Federation of Labor group that organized individual national unions of skilled workers

Samuel Gompers leader of the American Federation of Labor

collective bargaining workers acting together for better wages or working conditions

Mary Harris Jones union supporter who organized strikes and educated workers

Haymarket Riot a union protest in Chicago where strikers fought with police

Homestead strike violent 1892 strike of Carnegie steelworkers ended by state militia

Pullman strike strike of Pullman railroad workers that stopped traffic on many midwestern rail lines; ended in 1894 when federal troops were sent to stop it

Lesson Summary

MAXIMIZING PROFITS AND EFFICIENCY

During the Second Industrial Revolution, machines did more and more work. The unskilled workers who ran the machines could not complain about conditions. If they did, they could be replaced.

In the early 1900s efficiency engineer **Frederick W. Taylor** wrote a book that took a scientific look at how businesses could increase profits.

> What impact did Frederick Taylor's book have on America's workers?
>
> _____
>
> _____

One way was to ignore workers and their needs. As a result, conditions for workers got worse.

WORKERS ORGANIZE

Workers began to form labor unions. The **Knights of Labor** started out as a secret organization. However, by the end of the 1870s, the Knights became a national labor union. The head of the union was **Terence V. Powderly**. The Knights included both skilled and unskilled members.

The **American Federation of Labor**, under the leadership of **Samuel Gompers**, was different from the Knights of Labor. It organized national unions, and its members were all skilled workers.

Workers hoped that if they acted together using **collective bargaining**, they might be able to improve pay and working conditions.

Many women participated in unions. **Mary Harris Jones**, for example, helped organize strikes and educate workers.

LABOR STRIKES

In 1886 thousands of Chicago union members went on strike. After police killed two strikers, workers met at Haymarket Square to protest the killings. Someone threw a bomb, and police fired into the crowd. The **Haymarket Riot** ended with more than 100 people killed or wounded.

On June 29, 1892, at a Carnegie steel plant in Homestead, Pennsylvania, the **Homestead strike** began. Workers protested the introduction of new machinery and the loss of jobs. It ended in violence and death, and the union was defeated. Two years later, the **Pullman strike** was the result of layoffs and pay cuts. President Grover Cleveland sent federal troops to break the strike.

> Which union would have more power—a union of unskilled workers or a union of skilled workers?
>
> _____
> _____
> _____

> How did workers benefit from collective bargaining?
>
> _____
> _____

> Why do you think labor strikes often ended in violence?
>
> _____
> _____
> _____

CHALLENGE ACTIVITY

Critical Thinking: Explain Explain why workers
sometimes use strikes as a strategy.

DIRECTIONS Read each sentence and fill in the blank with the
word in the word pair that best completes the sentence.

1. _____ became the leader of the Knights of Labor and
   removed the secrecy surrounding it, making it the first national labor union
   in the United States. (Mary Harris Jones/Terence V. Powderly)

2. The _____, which occurred in 1892 at a Carnegie steel
   plant in Pennsylvania, resulted in violence and death and the defeat of the
   union. (Homestead strike/collective bargaining)

3. Union leaders tried to secure better wages and working conditions for
   all workers in a factory or industry through _____.
   (collective bargaining/Homestead strike)

4. _____ organized strikes and educated workers. (Mary
   Harris Jones/Samuel Gompers)

5. In 1886 two Chicago union members were killed while striking. When
   union members met to protest these killings, a clash known as the
   _____ was the result. (Pullman strike/Haymarket Riot)

6. As an efficiency engineer, _____ sought ways for
   businesses to increase profits. (Frederick W. Taylor/Terence V. Powderly)

7. Unlike other labor groups that allowed both skilled and unskilled laborers
   to join, the _____ led by _____
   limited its membership to skilled workers. (American Federation of Labor/
   Knights of Labor) (Mary Harris Jones/Samuel Gompers)

8. During the _____, workers refused to work on trains
   carrying Pullman cars, stopping traffic on many midwestern rail lines.
   (Homestead strike/Pullman strike)

9. The _____ was founded as a secret organization but
   became a national labor union by the end of the 1870s. (Knights of Labor/
   American Federation of Labor)

Immigrants and Urban Life

MAIN IDEAS
1. U.S. immigration patterns changed during the late 1800s as new immigrants arrived from Europe, Asia, and Mexico.
2. Immigrants worked hard to adjust to life in the United States.
3. Some Americans opposed immigration and worked to restrict it.

Key Terms and People

old immigrants people who arrived from northern Europe in the mid-1800s

new immigrants people who arrived from southern and eastern Europe in the late 1800s

steerage an area below a ship's deck where immigrants often traveled

benevolent societies organizations that offered help to immigrant families

sweatshops workplaces in small shops with poor working conditions and low pay

tenements poorly built, overcrowded apartment buildings

Chinese Exclusion Act law banning immigration by Chinese people for ten years

Lesson Summary
CHANGING PATTERNS OF IMMIGRATION

During the mid-1800s millions of immigrants came to the United States from northern Europe. Many of these **old immigrants** were skilled workers or farmers. Most were Protestants. Later, many **new immigrants** came from different places, including southern and eastern Europe. These immigrants came from many different cultures and religions.

Immigrants usually faced a difficult journey by ship to America, often traveling in **steerage**. Then they faced the challenge of actually getting into the United States. Many European immigrants entered at Ellis Island in New York Harbor. On the West Coast, many Chinese immigrants entered the United States through Angel Island near San Francisco. In the Southwest, Mexican immigrants came to the United States through El Paso, Texas.

> **Where did most of the new immigrants come from?**
> _____

> **Underline three points of entry for immigrants to the United States in the late 1800s.**

ADJUSTING TO A NEW LIFE

After entering the United States, immigrants had to adjust to life in a different country. They had to learn new customs and a new language. Many of them moved into neighborhoods with other people from the same country. Immigrant neighborhoods often had schools, clubs, newspapers, shops, and banks. These helped people start their new lives. **Benevolent societies** helped families in cases of sickness, unemployment, or death.

Many new immigrants came from rural areas. They lacked the skills to work in modern manufacturing or industrial jobs. As a result, many of them had to take low-paying unskilled manufacturing jobs in large factories and **sweatshops**. Their low-paying jobs often forced them to live in **tenements**.

> **Why did many immigrants have to take low-paying jobs in sweatshops?**
>
> _____
>
> _____
>
> _____

OPPOSITION TO IMMIGRATION

Some Americans welcomed new immigrants. Others feared that immigrants would take away jobs from native-born Americans. Some Americans called nativists believed that too many immigrants were being allowed into the country. This led to a growth in anti-immigrant feelings during the late 1800s.

Some nativists used violent means to show their anger toward immigrants. Some people advocated laws to limit immigration. Congress passed the **Chinese Exclusion Act**, which banned immigration from China for ten years. A later law restricted convicts, people who had certain diseases, and those likely to need public assistance. However, even with these laws, immigrants continued to arrive in large numbers.

> **What was the purpose of the Chinese Exclusion Act?**
>
> _____
>
> _____

CHALLENGE ACTIVITY

Critical Thinking: Explain Write a letter to the editor of a newspaper in the late 1880s. Explain

your opinion about limiting the number of
immigrants to the United States.

benevolent societies	new immigrants	steerage	tenements
Chinese Exclusion Act	old immigrants	sweatshops	

DIRECTIONS Match the terms in the first column with the correct
definitions from the second column by placing the letter of the
correct definition in the space provided before each term.

_____ 1. Chinese
           Exclusion Act

_____ 2. sweatshops

_____ 3. benevolent
           societies

_____ 4. steerage

_____ 5. old immigrants

_____ 6. new immigrants

_____ 7. tenements

a. immigrants from northern Europe

b. an area below a ship's deck where immigrants
   often traveled

c. poorly built, overcrowded apartment buildings

d. a law that banned Chinese people from
   immigrating to the United States for 10 years

e. workplaces in which employees endured long
   hours and hot, unhealthy working conditions

f. organizations that offered immigrant families
   help in cases of sickness, unemployment, or
   death

g. immigrants from southern and eastern Europe

DIRECTIONS Use the seven words or phrases from the word bank
to write a summary of what you learned in the lesson.

_____

_____

_____

_____

_____

_____

_____

Immigrants and Urban Life

Lesson 2

MAIN IDEAS
1. Both immigrants and native-born Americans moved to growing urban areas in record numbers in the late 1800s and early 1900s.
2. New technology and ideas helped cities change and adapt to rapid population growth.

Key Terms and People

mass transit public transportation designed to move a large number of people

suburbs residential neighborhoods outside of downtown areas

mass culture leisure and cultural activities shared by many people

Joseph Pulitzer publisher of *New York World* newspaper

William Randolph Hearst publisher of *New York Journal* newspaper

department stores large retail stores that sell many different types of goods

Frederick Law Olmsted landscape architect who designed Central Park in New York City

Lesson Summary
GROWTH OF URBAN AREAS

During the late 1800s many native-born Americans and immigrants moved to cities. By 1900 about 40 percent of Americans lived in cities. The people moving into large cities included new immigrants and rural residents looking for work. Farm equipment replaced workers in rural areas. African Americans from the rural South moved to northern cities. They wanted to escape discrimination and find better opportunities.

Between 1850 and 1900, Chicago grew from 30,000 people to 1.7 million. Many of the new residents were immigrants from southern and eastern Europe. One factor in the growth of Chicago was its location on new railroad lines. These rail lines placed Chicago in the center of the trade in lumber, grain, and meat.

Why did many African Americans move from southern farm areas to northern cities?
_____
_____

CHANGING CITIES

New technology helped cities grow quickly and changed the look of American cities. One way to find space for people to live and work was to build taller buildings. The steel industry grew in the late 1800s. Steel beams became inexpensive enough to use in frames of tall buildings. The invention of the safety elevator made skyscrapers practical.

Skyscrapers made it possible for more people to work and live in the cities. **Mass transit** developed, allowing people to travel in large numbers. Mass transit let many middle-class residents move to **suburbs**.

As the publishing industry grew, **mass culture** developed in the United States. Big cities often had many competing newspapers. **Joseph Pulitzer** published the *New York World*. He added a color comic to the paper. **William Randolph Hearst** published the *New York Journal*. When he realized his competitor was gaining readership, he added a color comic. Huge **department stores** changed the way people shopped for goods in cities.

The demand for public entertainment led to large fairs and the creation of amusement parks. People also needed open public space in large cities. **Frederick Law Olmsted** became famous for designing Central Park in New York City, as well as many state and national parks.

> **How did the development of mass transit lead to growth of suburbs?**
> _____
> _____
> _____

> **Television is part of today's mass culture. What are some other examples of things that are part of today's mass culture?**
> _____
> _____
> _____

> **Underline the sentence that explains why large fairs and amusement parks were developed.**

CHALLENGE ACTIVITY

Critical Thinking: Analyze During the second half of the nineteenth century, new inventions made farming much more efficient. How did these inventions promote the growth of cities?

DIRECTIONS Write two phrases that describe the term given. Include details you've learned from the lesson.

1. department stores _____
   _____

2. Frederick Law Olmsted _____

3. Joseph Pulitzer _____
   _____

4. mass culture _____
   _____

5. mass transit _____
   _____

6. suburbs _____
   _____

7. William Randolph Hearst _____
   _____

DIRECTIONS Read each sentence and fill in the blank with the word in the word pair that best completes the sentence.

8. _____, the publisher of the *New York World*, included a color comic in his paper. (William Randolph Hearst/ Joseph Pulitzer)

9. _____ is public transportation that moves a large number of people. (Mass transit/Mass culture)

10. The landscape architect who designed Central Park in New York City was _____. (William Randolph Hearst/ Frederick Law Olmsted)

MAIN IDEAS
1. Crowded urban areas faced a variety of social problems.
2. People worked to improve the quality of life in U.S. cities.

Key Terms and People

Jacob Riis journalist and photographer who exposed the horrible conditions in New York City tenements

settlement houses neighborhood centers in poor areas that offered education, recreation, and social activities

Jane Addams co-founder of Hull House

Hull House Chicago's most famous settlement house

assimilation process in which immigrant families adopted some American beliefs and aspects of American culture

Florence Kelley Chicago reformer who worked to pass child labor laws

Lesson Summary
URBAN PROBLEMS

Even with new technology, many cities were not ready for the population growth of the late 1800s. There was a shortage of affordable housing. This led to overcrowding and poor living conditions. Many poor families were squeezed into tiny tenement apartments. **Jacob Riis** became famous for his articles and photographs that exposed the horrible conditions in New York City tenements.

The overcrowding caused sanitation problems and unsafe living conditions. Garbage collection systems were not efficient. Garbage piled up in the cities. Indoor plumbing was scarce, and water supplies became polluted. Fires could spread rapidly and fire escapes were often blocked.

These conditions caused the spread of disease-causing bacteria. There were outbreaks of diseases such as typhoid, cholera, influenza, and tuberculosis. As a result, about half of the babies

> What did Jacob Riis do to help change conditions in tenement apartments?
>
> _____
>
> _____
>
> _____

> Underline the sentences that describe the sanitation problems caused by crowded conditions in cities.

Lesson 3, *continued*

born died before the age of five. The overcrowded living conditions and the manufacturing industries also caused serious air pollution problems.

City governments worked to reduce these problems by hiring firefighters and police officers. New sewage and drinking water purification systems helped reduce the sanitation problem.

What did cities do to relieve the health and safety problems caused by overcrowding?
_____
_____
_____

IMPROVING CITY LIFE

Reformers worked to improve living conditions in tenements. In 1901 new laws in New York State required better ventilation and running water in new buildings. Other states followed New York's lead.

Private organizations also helped the urban poor. Some people developed **settlement houses**. These settlement houses had professionals and volunteers on staff, including educated women from wealthy families. Some of these houses are still active today.

Jane Addams and Ellen Gates Starr moved into a rundown building and turned it into **Hull House** in Chicago. This was the most famous settlement house. The staff served the needs of immigrant families. They helped them in the process of **assimilation**. They provided English classes, day care, cooking and sewing classes, and other services.

How did Hull House staff help immigrants assimilate?
_____
_____
_____

The Hull House staff also worked for reforms to improve conditions for poor families. **Florence Kelley** visited sweatshops. Then she wrote about the problems she saw there. She helped convince lawmakers in Illinois to pass a law limiting work hours for women and preventing child labor. She later became the chief factory inspector for the state and helped enforce the law.

How did Florence Kelley get the government involved in improving conditions for women and children?
_____
_____
_____

CHALLENGE ACTIVITY

Critical Thinking: Analyze As cities grew rapidly, crowded conditions created many problems. Why didn't the people just move away from the cities to find better conditions?

assimilation	Hull House	Jane Addams
Florence Kelley	Jacob Riis	settlement houses

DIRECTIONS On the line provided before each statement, write **T** if a statement is true and **F** if a statement is false. If the statement is false, write the correct term on the line after each sentence that makes the sentence a true statement.

_____ 1. <u>Jane Addams</u> became famous for exposing the horrible conditions in New York City tenements.

_____

_____ 2. <u>Settlement houses</u> were neighborhood centers in poor areas that offered education, recreation, and social activities.

_____

_____ 3. Immigrants who adopted some American beliefs and aspects of American culture went through a process of <u>assimilation</u>.

_____

_____ 4. An important reformer at Hull House who visited sweatshops and wrote about the problem of child labor was <u>Jacob Riis</u>.

_____

_____ 5. <u>Jacob Riis</u> and Ellen Gates Starr in Chicago founded Hull House.

_____

_____ 6. <u>Hull House</u> was the most famous settlement house of its time and was known for helping immigrant families assimilate to life in the United States.

_____

The Progressive Spirit of Reform

MAIN IDEAS
1. Political corruption was common during the Gilded Age.
2. Progressives pushed for reforms to improve living conditions.
3. Progressive reforms expanded the voting power of citizens.

Key Terms and People

political machines powerful organizations that used both legal and illegal methods to get their candidates elected to public office

Progressives reformers who wanted to solve the problems of a fast-growing society

muckrakers journalists who exposed the corruption, scandal, and filth of society

Seventeenth Amendment a law letting Americans vote directly for U.S. senators

recall a vote to remove an official before the end of his or her term

initiative procedure allowing voters to propose a new law by collecting signatures on a petition

referendum procedure permitting voters to approve or reject a law

Robert M. La Follette Wisconsin governor whose progressive reforms became a model for other states

Lesson Summary
POLITICAL CORRUPTION

During the Gilded Age, governments were riddled with corruption. **Political machines** controlled most local politics. Illegal activities included buying votes, bribing vote counters, and stuffing ballot boxes with extra votes. Both of President Ulysses S. Grant's terms were very corrupt. Some members of Congress were involved in a railroad scandal. This caused widespread public distrust.

Many of the jobs with the civil service were given to political supporters rather than to qualified candidates. Presidents Hayes and Garfield tried to reform civil service. President

> **What illegal activities did political machines use to change election results?**
>
> _____
> _____
> _____

Chester Arthur signed an act requiring civil
service tests to prove applicants were qualified.

PROGRESSIVES PUSH FOR REFORMS

Progressives were reformers. They wanted to
solve problems caused by the fast urban growth
of the late 1800s. Journalists wrote articles about
such issues as child labor, racial discrimination,
and slum housing. Called **muckrakers** for the
scandals they exposed, these writers encouraged
reforms. Upton Sinclair wrote about unsanitary
practices in the meat-processing industry. Lincoln
Steffens exposed corruption in city government.

Many Progressives helped the urban poor. This
led to improved conditions in cities. Other
progressive leaders focused on education. States
passed laws requiring children to attend school.
Kindergartens opened to teach children basic
social skills. John Dewey was a supporter of
education. His motive was to help children use
problem-solving skills, not just memorization.
Education reform also improved the medical
profession.

> **What does the term *muckraker* mean?**
> _____
> _____
> _____

EXPANSION OF VOTING POWER

Reformers hoped to expand voting power. They
favored the direct primary, in which voters
choose candidates directly. They also favored the
Seventeenth Amendment. This allowed Americans
to vote for U.S. senators directly. **Recall** votes
removed officials before the end of their terms. In
some states voters proposed laws with **initiatives**.
Some states let **referendums** overrule laws.

Wisconsin governor **Robert M. La Follette**
challenged the power of political machines. His
reform plan became known as the Wisconsin
Idea, and it was used as a model for reform in
other states.

> **What does the Seventeenth Amendment allow Americans to do?**
> _____
> _____

> **Who developed the Wisconsin Idea?**
> _____

CHALLENGE ACTIVITY

Critical Thinking: Sequence Make a timeline of
the presidents who served the United States
during the Gilded Age.

DIRECTIONS Look at each set of terms below. On the line provided,
write the letter of the term that does not relate to the others.

_____ 1. a. political machine
        b. muckrakers
        c. recall
        d. initiative

_____ 3. a. Robert M. La Follette
        b. political machines
        c. Progressives
        d. Upton Sinclair

_____ 2. a. muckrakers
        b. recall
        c. Seventeenth Amendment
        d. referendum

_____ 4. a. initiative
        b. reform measures
        c. referendum
        d. exploration

DIRECTIONS Write two descriptive phrases that describe the term,
person, or event.

5. political machines _____

_____

6. Seventeenth Amendment _____

_____

7. muckrakers _____

_____

8. initiative _____

_____

9. Progressives _____

_____

The Progressive Spirit of Reform

MAIN IDEAS
1. Reformers attempted to improve conditions for child laborers.
2. Unions and reformers took steps to improve safety in the workplace and to limit working hours.

Key Terms and People

Triangle Shirtwaist Fire tragic fire that killed 146 workers

workers' compensation laws guarantee a portion of lost wages to workers injured on the job; first passed in1902 in Maryland

capitalism economic system in which private businesses run most industries and competition determines how much goods cost

socialism system in which government owns and operates a country's industry

William "Big Bill" Haywood union leader of the Industrial Workers of the World

Industrial Workers of the World labor union founded in 1905 on socialist beliefs

Lesson Summary
IMPROVING CONDITIONS FOR CHILDREN

Reformers also focused on child labor. Children worked in a variety of jobs. Some sold newspapers. Some took care of boarders at their homes. Some sewed clothing. Many worked in industry in factories, mines, and mills. Sometimes children as young as seven were sent to work in these places. They earned very low wages.

Florence Kelley was a reformer who got involved in child labor. She was a board member of the National Consumers' League. The league spoke out on labor issues involving women and children. In 1912 Massachusetts became the first state to pass a minimum wage law. Congress, too, tried to pass laws protecting working children. However, the Supreme Court ruled many of these laws unconstitutional.

> **How do you think a minimum wage law helped protect children?**
> _____
> _____

SAFETY AND WORKING CONDITIONS

Progressives also fought to ensure workers' safety, limit working hours, and protect workers' rights. It took several terrible accidents before laws ensuring workers' safety were passed. One of the worst was the **Triangle Shirtwaist Fire** in New York City. When the factory caught fire, many workers died because factory owners had locked the exit doors.

Reformers also concentrated on getting **workers' compensation laws** passed. These laws guarantee a portion of lost wages to employees who are injured on the job. Some business leaders believed that the economy should operate without government influence. So laws were not always enforced. In *Lochner* v. *New York*, the Supreme Court ruled that states could not restrict the types of labor agreements between employers and employees. The Supreme Court did, however, put limits on the number of hours women and children could work.

Labor unions also tried to improve working conditions. Some wanted to take drastic measures, such as changing the economic system of the country to socialism. In **capitalism**, private businesses run most industries and competition determines how much goods cost and how much workers are paid. Under **socialism**, the government owns all the means of production. A new union, based on socialist ideas, was founded in 1905. Under its leader, **William "Big Bill" Haywood**, the **Industrial Workers of the World** (IWW) hoped to overthrow capitalism. It tried industrial sabotage but was not successful and had declined by 1920.

What finally motivated leaders to pass laws ensuring workers' safety?
_____
_____
_____

What is the purpose of workers' compensation laws?
_____
_____
_____

How was the Industrial Workers of the World different from other labor unions?
_____
_____
_____

CHALLENGE ACTIVITY

Critical Thinking: Make Judgments Make a list of the different ways your life would be changed if the reforms discussed here had not happened.

Use this list to decide whether you agree with the reforms.

capitalism	Triangle Shirtwaist Fire
Industrial Workers of the World	workers' compensation laws
socialism	

DIRECTIONS Use the five words or phrases from the word list to write a summary of what you learned in the lesson.

_____

_____

_____

_____

_____

DIRECTIONS Write three descriptive phrases that describe the term given.

1. capitalism _____

_____

2. socialism _____

_____

3. William "Big Bill" Haywood _____

_____

4. Industrial Workers of the World _____

_____

5. Triangle Shirtwaist Fire _____

_____

6. workers' compensation laws _____

_____

The Progressive Spirit of Reform

Lesson 3

MAIN IDEAS
1. Women fought for temperance and the right to vote.
2. African American reformers challenged discrimination and called for equality.
3. Progressive reforms failed to benefit all minorities.

Key Terms and People

Eighteenth Amendment amendment banning production and sale of alcoholic drinks

National American Woman Suffrage Association group that worked for women's voting rights, founded by Elizabeth Cady Stanton and Susan B. Anthony

Alice Paul founder of a women's suffrage group that became the National Woman's Party

Nineteenth Amendment amendment giving women the right to vote

Booker T. Washington African American educator who encouraged other African Americans to improve their own lives rather than fight discrimination

Ida B. Wells African American journalist who publicized lynchings in her newspaper

W. E. B. Du Bois African American reformer who publicized cases of racial prejudice

National Association for the Advancement of Colored People (NAACP) civil rights organization that works for racial equality by using the courts

Lesson Summary
WOMEN FIGHT FOR TEMPERANCE AND VOTING RIGHTS

New educational opportunities opened up for women in the late 1800s. However, many male-dominated fields were still closed to women. Women's reform groups focused on two issues. One was the right to vote. The other was temperance, for many believed alcohol caused many of society's problems.

In 1874 the Women's Christian Temperance Union was formed. This group fought for laws restricting alcohol sales. Their efforts met with success in 1919 when the **Eighteenth Amendment** banned the production and sale of alcohol.

> **What was the purpose of the Women's Christian Temperance Union?**
> _____
> _____

Lesson 3, *continued*

Meanwhile, women struggled for the right to vote. By 1890 some western states had given women suffrage. That year, the **National American Woman Suffrage Association** was founded. Carrie Chapman Catt became its president in 1900. She organized more than 1 million volunteers. **Alice Paul** founded what would become the National Woman's Party. Paul and other reformers were put in jail for their actions. In 1920 the **Nineteenth Amendment** gave women the right to vote.

> **What did the Nineteenth Amendment to the Constitution address?**
>
> _____
>
> _____

AFRICAN AMERICANS CHALLENGE DISCRIMINATION

African Americans had won their freedom, but they still faced discrimination and segregation. African American educator **Booker T. Washington** urged African Americans to focus on education and economic well-being to end discrimination. **Ida B. Wells** drew attention to the lynching of African Americans. In her newspaper, *Free Speech,* she referred to lynching as "our country's national crime." **W. E. B. Du Bois** believed that African Americans should protest unjust treatment and fight for equal rights. He and others founded the **National Association for the Advancement of Colored People** to show the struggles of African Americans. The National Urban League helped blacks find jobs and housing in northern cities.

> **Underline the names of all the reformers identified in this section.**

FAILURES OF REFORM

Chinese and Mexican immigrants and Native Americans were left out by many reforms. In 1911 the Society of Native Americans was founded to fight Indian poverty. Some Native Americans felt that adopting the ways of whites was destroying their heritage. Chinese immigrants faced discrimination and hard lives. Labor laws did not help Mexican immigrants. They did help the western and southwestern economies.

> **List three groups of people that were not generally helped by Progressive reforms.**
>
> _____
>
> _____
>
> _____

CHALLENGE ACTIVITY

Critical Thinking: Explain Research the
Eighteenth Amendment and its repeal. Then
write a paragraph about your findings.

DIRECTIONS Read each sentence and fill in the blank with the
word in the word pair that best completes the sentence.

1. Women were given the right to vote by the _____.
   (Eighteenth Amendment/Nineteenth Amendment)

2. _____ published the newspaper *Free Speech* and wrote
   about discrimination. (Ida B. Wells/Booker T. Washington)

3. _____ studied racial prejudice and pushed for protest
   against unjust treatment. (Alice Paul/W. E. B. Du Bois)

4. More than 1 million volunteers worked to broaden the right to vote as
   part of the _____. (National
   American Woman Suffrage Association/National Association for the
   Advancement of Colored People)

5. _____ was jailed for supporting women's suffrage. (Alice
   Paul/Ida B. Wells)

DIRECTIONS On the line provided before each statement, write **T** if
a statement is true and **F** if a statement is false. If the statement is
false, write the correct term on the line after each sentence that
makes the sentence a true statement.

_____ 6. The Nineteenth Amendment banned the sale of alcohol in 1919.

   _____

_____ 7. Booker T. Washington believed African Americans should not fight
   discrimination directly.

   _____

_____ 8. Ida B. Wells called lynching "our country's national crime."

   _____

_____ 9. The NAACP fought its battles against discrimination in the courts.

   _____

The Progressive Spirit of Reform

MAIN IDEAS
1. Theodore Roosevelt's progressive reforms tried to balance the interests of business, consumers, and laborers.
2. William Howard Taft angered Progressives with his cautious reforms, while Woodrow Wilson enacted far-reaching banking and antitrust reforms.

Key Terms and People

Theodore Roosevelt vice-president who became president upon McKinley's death

Pure Food and Drug Act law stopping the manufacture, sale, or transportation of mislabeled or contaminated food and drugs

conservation protection of nature and its resources

William Howard Taft president elected in 1908

Progressive Party nicknamed the Bull Moose Party; formed so Roosevelt could run for president in 1912

Woodrow Wilson Democratic president who worked to regulate tariffs, banking, and business

Sixteenth Amendment amendment that allows the federal government to impose direct taxes on people's incomes

Lesson Summary
ROOSEVELT'S PROGRESSIVE REFORMS

Vice-President **Theodore Roosevelt** became president when President McKinley was assassinated. Roosevelt was a progressive president. He believed the interests of businesses, workers, and consumers should be balanced, or even-sided. This policy was called the Square Deal.

During a 1902 coal miner strike, Roosevelt forced mine managers and strikers to settle their dispute. This was done through arbitration, a formal way of settling an argument. Roosevelt's Square Deal idea helped him win the 1904 election.

> **What did Theodore Roosevelt mean when he used the term *Square Deal*?**
>
> _____
> _____
> _____

President Roosevelt made regulating big business a top goal. Muckrakers helped him by focusing public attention on industry problems. One muckraker, Upton Sinclair, wrote a book on meat processing. The terrible conditions he described led to a meat-inspection law. His book also led to the **Pure Food and Drug Act** of 1906.

Roosevelt was the first president to consider **conservation** an important national issue. Some people such as John Muir wanted nature to be preserved for its beauty. Others wanted to make sure natural resources were used efficiently. Nearly 150 million acres of public land was saved from development during Roosevelt's presidency.

> **What were some reasons people supported conservation?**
> _____
> _____
> _____

REFORMS OF TAFT AND WILSON

William Howard Taft became president in 1908 with Roosevelt's support. He felt Roosevelt had more power than the Constitution allowed. So he moved toward reform slowly. Various Progressives, including Roosevelt, were not satisfied with some of his reforms. In 1912 Roosevelt formed and ran with the **Progressive Party** against Taft. However, Democrat **Woodrow Wilson** won.

> **Why did Theodore Roosevelt form a third party for the 1912 elections?**
> _____
> _____

President Wilson immediately began to push for certain reforms. He was especially interested in tariffs and banking. His reforms led to passage of the **Sixteenth Amendment**, allowing a direct income tax.

Wilson worked to regulate banking with the Federal Reserve Act in 1913. Passage of the Clayton Antitrust Act and the creation of the Federal Trade Commission helped regulate big business. These programs also helped Wilson win reelection in 1916.

> **What was the purpose of the Federal Trade Commission?**
> _____

CHALLENGE ACTIVITY

Critical Thinking: Evaluate Write a short paragraph explaining how muckrakers played an

important role in the reforms backed by U.S.
presidents.

DIRECTIONS Match the terms in the first column with their correct
definitions from the second column by placing the letter of the
correct definition in the space provided before each term.

_____ 1. Theodore Roosevelt

_____ 2. Pure Food and Drug Act

_____ 3. conservation

_____ 4. William Howard Taft

_____ 5. Progressive Party

_____ 6. Woodrow Wilson

_____ 7. Sixteenth Amendment

a. the protection of nature and its resources

b. formed by Theodore Roosevelt in 1912 to challenge President Taft

c. believed the interests of businesspeople and laborers should be balanced for the public good

d. won the election of 1912 after the Republican vote was split between two other candidates

e. allowed the government to impose taxes directly on citizens' incomes

f. law that prohibited the sale of mislabeled or contaminated food and drugs

g. followed Theodore Roosevelt as president but upset many Progressives

DIRECTIONS Read each sentence and fill in the blank with the
word in the word pair that best completes the sentence.

8. President _____ was the first president to consider
   conservation an important national issue. (Theodore Roosevelt/William
   Howard Taft)

9. President _____ pushed for reforms dealing with tariffs
   and banking. (William Howard Taft /Woodrow Wilson)

10. Pressure from muckrakers led to the passage of the _____.
    (Pure Food and Drug Act /Sixteenth Amendment)

America as a World Power

MAIN IDEAS
1. The United States ended its policy of isolationism and began imperial expansion.
2. Hawaii became a United States territory in 1898.
3. The United States sought trade with Japan and China.

Key Terms and People

imperialism building an empire by founding colonies or conquering other nations

isolationism a policy of avoiding involvement in the affairs of other countries

William H. Seward secretary of state who arranged for the purchase of Alaska

Liliuokalani Hawaiian queen who proposed a new constitution that gave power back to Hawaiians in 1893

spheres of influence areas where foreign nations control trade and natural resources

Open Door Policy policy stating that all nations should have equal access to trade in China

Boxer Rebellion a rebellion led by a group of Chinese nationalists who were angered by foreign involvement in China

Lesson Summary
END OF ISOLATION

The decades surrounding 1900 were a time of **imperialism**. During those years, Europeans built great empires by taking control of other lands.

At first the United States followed a policy of **isolationism**. It did this to avoid conflicts and getting involved with the affairs of other countries. That changed in 1867 when Secretary of State **William H. Seward** purchased Alaska. This new territory was a valuable source of fur, minerals, timber, and gold. The United States then took the Midway Islands, part of Samoa, and Hawaii.

> Why would the United States favor isolationism?
>
> _____
>
> _____

HAWAII BECOMES A TERRITORY

Americans became rich sugar planters, shop owners, and shipyard owners. Sugar became a leading export in Hawaii. In 1887 the planters forced the king to sign the Bayonet Constitution, It gave more power to the planter-controlled parliament. Then Queen **Liliuokalani** proposed returning Hawaii to the Hawaiians. The United States sent marines to take control of the islands.

> **How did the United States take control of Hawaii?**
> _____

UNITED STATES SEEKS TRADE WITH JAPAN AND CHINA

The United States sent Commodore Matthew Perry to open trade relations with Japan. In 1858 the United States and Japan signed a trade agreement. Ten years later, Japanese leaders who favored the process of industrialization came into power. They began a 40-year period of change.

The Japanese attacked China and defeated them in 1894 to became a major world power. Afterwards, other countries took advantage of China's weakness to set up **spheres of influence**. To make sure it could trade with China, Secretary of State John Hay announced the **Open Door Policy**. This policy said that all nations should have an equal chance to trade with China.

> **How did Japan become a major world power?**
> _____
> _____

Chinese resentment grew because the Chinese did not like being controlled by foreigners. In 1900 this resentment exploded in the **Boxer Rebellion**. The Boxers attacked the areas where foreigners lived.

For two months the Boxers laid siege to the settlement. Then, military forces from several nations arrived and defeated the Boxers. China was forced to pay $333 million to various nations, and the Open Door Policy remained in effect for years.

> **Why were the Boxers unhappy with foreigners in China?**
> _____
> _____

CHALLENGE ACTIVITY

Critical Thinking: Evaluate On a map, locate the Midway Islands, Samoa, and Hawaii. Write a

Lesson 1, *continued*

paragraph evaluating why the United States
wanted to control these islands.

imperialism	spheres of influence	isolationism
Open Door Policy	William H. Seward	Boxer Rebellion
Liliuokalani	process	

DIRECTIONS Use five of the words or phrases from the word list to
write a summary of what you learned in the lesson.

_____

_____

_____

_____

_____

_____

DIRECTIONS Look at each set of terms below. On the line provided,
write the letter of the term that does not relate to the others.

_____ 1. a. Matthew Perry
       b. William H. Seward
       c. George Washington
       d. John Hay

_____ 2. a. Liliuokalani
       b. Open Door Policy
       c. Boxer Rebellion
       d. spheres of influence

_____ 3. a. economic interest
       b. naval bases
       c. imperialism
       d. isolationism

_____ 4. a. spheres of influence
       b. Alaska
       c. Boxer Rebellion
       d. China

America as a World Power

MAIN IDEAS
1. In 1898 the United States went to war with Spain in the Spanish-American War.
2. The United States gained territories in the Caribbean and Pacific.

Key Terms and People

yellow journalism technique that exaggerates and sensationalizes news stories

Teller Amendment war resolution amendment stating that the United States had no interest in taking control of Cuba

Emilio Aguinaldo leader of Filipino rebels against Spain

Anti-Imperialist League organization that opposed the creation of an American colonial empire and involvement in the affairs of Cuba and other island territories

Platt Amendment amendment to Cuba's constitution that limited Cuba's rights and kept the United States involved in Cuban affairs

Lesson Summary
WAR WITH SPAIN

During the 1890s Cuba rebelled against Spain, and many Americans were sympathetic to the Cubans. Two Americans who supported the rebellion were Joseph Pulitzer and William Randolph Hearst, powerful newspaper publishers. They used **yellow journalism** and published exaggerated stories. This technique sold more newspapers and increased American support for Cuba.

Hearst published a letter in which a Spanish official referred to President McKinley as weak. Many Americans were insulted. Before that, the U.S. battleship *Maine* had exploded in Cuba's Havana Harbor. No one knew the cause, but many Americans believed that Spain was responsible.

In response, the U.S. Congress declared that Cuba was an independent country. They also

> Why did publishers such as Pulitzer and Hearst resort to yellow journalism?
>
> _____
>
> _____
>
> _____

passed the **Teller Amendment**, which stated that America would not take control of Cuba. Spain immediately declared war and fighting began in Cuba.

The U.S. began fighting in the Philippines, a Spanish colony in the Pacific. General Dewey and the U.S. Navy destroyed Spain's fleet. Filipino rebels led by **Emilio Aguinaldo** then helped them take control of Manila, the capital.

Other U.S. troops focused on the Caribbean Sea. These troops included the Rough Riders, led by future President Theodore Roosevelt. After the United States won battles both on land (in Cuba and Puerto Rico) and at sea, Spain surrendered.

> **Why was the war fought in the Pacific as well as in Cuba?**
> _____
> _____

> **Why would Filipinos want to help the United States fight the Spanish?**
> _____
> _____

UNITED STATES GAINS TERRITORIES

The peace treaty with Spain put Cuba, Guam, Puerto Rico, and the Philippines under U.S. control. A group of Americans formed the **Anti-Imperialist League**. The group feared the United States wanted to build an empire and deny self-government to the territories. Despite its work, the treaty passed.

The United States set up a military government in Cuba and added the **Platt Amendment** to Cuba's new constitution. This allowed the United States to stay involved in Cuba's affairs and limited Cuba's right to make treaties. The amendment remained in force until 1934. The United States stayed active in Cuban affairs until the late 1950s.

The U.S. decided to keep the Philippines and Puerto Rico as territories. Puerto Ricans became U.S. citizens in 1917. Today, Puerto Rico has its own constitution, but it is still associated with the U.S. Filipinos fought for their independence, and in 1902 Congress established an appointed governor and elected legislature in the Philippines. The country gained independence in 1946.

> **Why did many Americans oppose the U.S. control of more land?**
> _____
> _____
> _____

CHALLENGE ACTIVITY

Critical Thinking: Compare Write a paragraph that compares the purpose of the Teller Amendment with the purpose of the Platt Amendment.

DIRECTIONS Read each sentence and fill in the blank with the word in the word pair that best completes the sentence.

1. The _____ opposed U.S. creation of a colonial empire and its control over Cuba and other island territories. (Teller Amendment/Anti-Imperialist League)

2. When William Randolph Hearst printed sensational or exaggerated news stories, he was practicing _____. (yellow journalism/the Platt Amendment)

3. The _____ limited Cuba's independence and gave the United States the right to intervene in its political affairs. (Teller Amendment/Platt Amendment)

4. The assistance of _____ allowed the U.S. Army to defeat the Spanish in the Philippines. (Teller Amendment/Emilio Aguinaldo)

5. The _____ was part of a war resolution that said the United States had no interest in controlling Cuba. (Teller Amendment/Platt Amendment)

DIRECTIONS On the line provided before each statement, write **T** if a statement is true and **F** if a statement is false. If the statement is false, write the correct term on the line after each sentence that makes the statement a true statement.

_____ 6. Dewey was helped by <u>Dr. Walter Reed</u> in conquering the Philippines.

_____

_____ 7. <u>Yellow journalism</u> led many Americans to support the Cuban rebels.

_____

_____ 8. The <u>Teller Amendment</u> indicated that the U.S. government was not interested in building an empire in Cuba.

_____

_____ 9. The <u>Teller Amendment</u> allowed the U.S. to stay involved in Cuba's affairs and limited Cuba's right to make treaties.

_____

America as a World Power

MAIN IDEAS
1. The United States built the Panama Canal in the early 1900s.
2. Theodore Roosevelt changed U.S. policy toward Latin America.
3. Presidents Taft and Wilson promoted U.S. interests in Latin America.

Key Terms and People

Panama Canal canal built in Panama that shortened the Atlantic-to-Pacific voyage

Roosevelt Corollary President Theodore Roosevelt's warning that nations in the Western Hemisphere should pay their debts and "behave"

dollar diplomacy President William Howard Taft's policy of influencing governments through economic intervention rather than military intervention

Mexican Revolution violent rebellion against Mexican president Porfirio Díaz

John J. Pershing United States general who pursued Pancho Villa through Mexico but never caught him

Francisco "Pancho" Villa rebel leader during the Mexican Revolution

Lesson Summary
BUILDING THE PANAMA CANAL

A canal across Central America would cut 8,000 miles off a voyage between the east and west coasts of the U.S. It would link the country's naval fleets. When Theodore Roosevelt became president, he tried to get Colombia to lease land in Panama for a canal. Colombia rejected the idea.

When Panama revolted against Colombia in 1903, a U.S. warship blocked Colombian forces from reaching Panama. The rebels won, and Panama declared itself independent. Then the United States and Panama agreed to build a canal.

Many lives were lost to disease and dangerous conditions during the construction of the **Panama Canal**. Despite these dangers, it opened in 1914.

> Why would foreign nations be interested in building a canal through Central America?
>
> _____
> _____
> _____

U.S. POLICY TOWARD LATIN AMERICA

In 1823 President Monroe warned European
nations to stay out of the Western Hemisphere.
The Monroe Doctrine became a major part of
U.S. foreign policy until 1904. When Theodore
Roosevelt became president, he wanted the
United States to play a more active role in the
Western Hemisphere.

By the early 1900s several Latin American
nations owed money to European investors.
Roosevelt warned these nations that if they did
not pay their debts, the United States would step
in. The **Roosevelt Corollary** was an addition to
the Monroe Doctrine. It gave the United States
"police power" in the Western Hemisphere.

> **How is the Roosevelt Corollary related to the Monroe Doctrine?**
>
> _____
>
> _____
>
> _____

U.S. INTERESTS IN LATIN AMERICA

President William Howard Taft tried **dollar
diplomacy**. This was a way to influence
governments by economic means rather than
through military means. Woodrow Wilson did
not like the role of big business in foreign affairs.
He ended the use of dollar diplomacy. Then he
sent troops to protect U.S. interests in Latin
America.

> **What would be an advantage of dollar diplomacy over military intervention?**
>
> _____
>
> _____

In 1910 the **Mexican Revolution** caused the
overthrow of the government. The violence of
the revolution caused many Mexicans to flee to
the United States. It also upset American
business leaders who had investments in Mexico.
President Woodrow Wilson requested and
received from Congress permission to use force
against Mexico.

> **Underline the sentence that states why many Mexicans moved to the United States in the early twentieth century.**

Wilson sent General **John J. Pershing** and
15,000 soldiers into Mexico to catch **Francisco
"Pancho" Villa**, the rebel leader. Villa had killed
17 Americans in New Mexico. Pershing and his
troops never caught Villa. In 1917 a new
constitution started to bring order to Mexico.

CHALLENGE ACTIVITY

Critical Thinking: Summarize Write a paragraph
that relates the attempts U.S. presidents made to
control Latin America.

DIRECTIONS Match the terms in the first column with their correct
definitions from the second column by placing the letter of the
correct definition in the space provided before each term.

_____ 1. Panama Canal

_____ 2. Roosevelt Corollary

_____ 3. dollar diplomacy

_____ 4. Mexican Revolution

_____ 5. John J. Pershing

_____ 6. Francisco "Pancho" Villa

a. stated that "wrongdoing" by Latin American countries could lead to U.S. intervention

b. a violent struggle beginning in 1910 that led to U.S. military intervention

c. led U.S. troops into Mexico in a failed mission

d. reduced travel times for cargo ships

e. attempted to influence Latin American governments with economic, not military, intervention

f. rebel leader who eluded U.S. troops in Mexico

DIRECTIONS Write two adjectives or descriptive phrases that
describe the term given.

7. Panama Canal _____

_____

8. Roosevelt Corollary _____

_____

9. dollar diplomacy _____

_____

10. Mexican Revolution _____

_____

World War I

MAIN IDEAS
1. Many factors contributed to the outbreak of World War I.
2. European nations suffered massive casualties in the war's early battles.

Key Terms and People

militarism aggressive strengthening of armed forces

Archduke Francis Ferdinand heir to the throne of Austria-Hungary who was assassinated in 1914

mobilized prepare military for war

Central powers alliance of Austria-Hungary and Germany at the start of the war

Allied powers alliance among France, Russia, and Britain at the start of the war

trench warfare defending a position by fighting from deep ditches

stalemate situation in which neither side can win a decisive victory

U-boats submarines used by the German navy in World War I

Lesson Summary
OUTBREAK OF WAR

Even though Europe was at peace in the early 1900s, there was a dangerous tension. One reason for this tension was nationalism. People who shared a language and culture wanted to unite. In some places such as Germany, nationalism brought stability, while in other places such as Austria-Hungary, it caused instability.

Another source of tension in Europe was imperialism. There was competition for territory in Europe and around the world. Nations began to focus on **militarism** and sought protection by forming new alliances.

As tensions grew, it became clear that a small "spark" could cause hostilities in Europe. The spark came when **Archduke Francis Ferdinand**

> Underline the sentence that describes the different effects of nationalism.

> What caused hostilities in Europe to erupt?
>
> _____
> _____
> _____

was assassinated by a Serbian nationalist. Austria-Hungary declared war on Serbia.

Alliances caused other countries to be drawn into the conflict. The opposing sides **mobilized** their armies. The **Central powers**, along with Bulgaria and the Ottoman Empire, faced the **Allied powers** and Italy. Soldiers from 30 nations on six continents would take part in the Great War, later known as World War I.

What countries fought along with the Central powers?
_____
_____

EARLY BATTLES OF THE WAR

Both sides expected a short war but the German army met strong resistance in Belgium. Two fronts developed. One was the western front, from the North Sea to Switzerland. The other was the eastern front, from the Black Sea to the Baltic Sea.

Trench warfare extended the battles. Soldiers died of injuries and disease as the two sides fought for months without gaining ground. New technology made the war deadlier than previous wars. Machine guns, artillery guns, and poison gas killed many soldiers. Tanks and airplanes were used in warfare for the first time.

How did new technology make World War I more deadly than previous wars?
_____
_____
_____

After a year the war had become a **stalemate**. Both sides launched massive attacks, and nearly 1 million men were killed. Still, neither side advanced very far.

Battles at sea were also very important. The British navy blockaded the Central powers' ports and laid explosive mines. The Germans used **U-boats** to launch torpedoes against Allied supply ships. The Germans also attacked ships from neutral countries that they believed were helping the Allies.

Why did the German navy attack ships from neutral countries?
_____
_____

CHALLENGE ACTIVITY

Critical Thinking: Analyze Write a short paragraph explaining how the building of alliances in Europe could make the continent less stable.

Lesson 1, *continued*

DIRECTIONS Write two words or phrases that describe each term below. Include details from the lesson.

1. militarism _____

_____

2. Central powers _____

_____

3. Allied powers _____

_____

4. trench warfare _____

_____

5. U-boats _____

_____

Allied powers	militarism	trench warfare
Archduke Francis Ferdinand	mobilize	U-boats
Central powers	stalemate	

DIRECTIONS Use five terms from the word bank to write a summary of what you learned in the lesson.

_____

_____

_____

_____

_____

_____

Lesson 2

MAIN IDEAS
1. The United States entered the war after repeated crises with Germany.
2. The United States mobilized for war by training troops and stepping up production of supplies.
3. Labor shortages created new wartime opportunities for women and other Americans.

Key Terms and People

Lusitania British passenger ship sunk by a German U-boat in 1915

Zimmermann Note secret telegram from the German foreign minister Arthur Zimmermann to Mexico proposing an alliance against the United States

Selective Service Act law that required men between the ages of 21 and 30 to register to be drafted into military service

Liberty bonds bonds issued to raise billions of dollars for the Allies' war efforts

National War Labor Board agency formed in 1918 to help settle labor disputes and avoid strikes during the war

Lesson Summary
THE UNITED STATES ENTERS WORLD WAR I
Many Americans were immigrants or children of immigrants from Europe. Even so, they wanted the country to remain neutral in the European conflict.

German U-boats attacked ships carrying supplies to the Allies. Then they began attacking passenger ships, such as the *Lusitania*, and American vessels. When Americans found out about the **Zimmermann Note**, they were outraged. President Woodrow Wilson asked Congress to declare war on Germany. War was declared on April 6, 1917.

> Circle the name of a non-combat ship sunk by the Germans during World War I.

> How did Americans react after they learned about the Zimmermann Note?
>
> _____
> _____

MOBILIZING FOR WAR
Rallies were held to build support as the country prepared for war. However, some freedoms, such as freedom of speech, were limited, and opponents of the war were jailed.

The **Selective Service Act** was passed in 1917 to prepare the military for war. Almost 3 million Americans, including many African Americans, were drafted into service. War preparations were very expensive, so money was raised through the sale of **Liberty bonds**.

The government took other actions to provide supplies for the troops. Metals, cement, and rubber were produced. Farmers got price guarantees to increase crops. Citizens were encouraged to use less food and to grow their own.

> **How were so many men enrolled in the military during World War I?**
> _____
> _____

NEW WARTIME OPPORTUNITIES

American factories needed to run work nonstop to produce weapons and supplies; however, the war cut off immigration, and many young men were fighting in Europe. These factors combined to create a labor shortage in the United States. Labor shortages led to new opportunities for many workers. More than 1 million women worked in factories, and others helped in Europe.

> **Why did so many more women work in factories during the war than before the war?**
> _____
> _____

Even with many women workers, factories needed more people. Mexican Americans from the West and African Americans from the South moved to northern industrial cities. Because labor was scarce, workers could demand better conditions. Union membership increased.

President Wilson set up the **National War Labor Board** in 1918. It settled disputes between workers and management. The board also helped establish a minimum wage and limited work hours, and it required fair pay for women.

> **Why were workers able to demand better working conditions?**
> _____
> _____
> _____

CHALLENGE ACTIVITY

Critical Thinking: Identify Cause and Effect Write a paragraph explaining how the need for military supplies led to a migration of people to northern cities.

DIRECTIONS Look at each set of terms below. On the line provided, write the letter of the term that does not relate to the others.

_____ 1. a. *Lusitania*
      b. U-boats
      c. passenger liner
      d. Zimmermann Note

_____ 2. a. war bond
      b. telegram
      c. Mexico
      d. Zimmermann Note

_____ 3. a. register
      b. National War Labor Board
      c. Selective Service Act
      d. army

_____ 4. a. Liberty bonds
      b. funding
      c. taxes
      d. *Lusitania*

_____ 5. a. unions
      b. National War Labor Board
      c. Liberty bonds
      d. work force

DIRECTIONS On the line provided before each statement, write **T** if a statement is true and **F** if a statement is false. If the statement is false, write the correct term on the line after each sentence that makes the sentence a true statement.

_____ 6. The <u>Selective Service Act</u> brought millions of men into the U.S. military.

_____

_____ 7. <u>Liberty bonds</u> were loans that helped to fund the war.

_____

_____ 8. The <u>*Lusitania*</u> was a secret telegram sent from Germany to Mexico.

_____

_____ 9. The <u>Selective Service Act</u> helped establish a minimum wage, limited work hours, and required fair pay for women.

_____

_____ 10. The <u>Zimmermann Note</u> pushed Americans toward war with Germany.

_____

World War I

MAIN IDEAS
1. American soldiers started to arrive in Europe in 1917.
2. The Americans helped the Allies win the war.
3. Germany agreed to an armistice after suffering heavy losses.

Key Terms and People

American Expeditionary Force U.S. troops sent to Europe during World War I

Communists people who favor the equal distribution of wealth and the end of all forms of private property

armistice truce between opponents that ends hostilities

Lesson Summary
AMERICAN SOLDIERS ARRIVE

The Allies were near defeat when U.S. troops began to arrive in Europe in 1917. French and British generals wanted the **American Expeditionary Force** to go to the front lines right away. General John J. Pershing, the commander of the American troops, insisted that they fight as a separate force. He did not want to spread American troops among Allied forces. He also insisted on completing training before sending soldiers into battle. He wanted them to be able to help achieve victory.

The Allies lost the help of Russia after **Communists** seized power in late 1917. The new leaders of Russia signed a peace agreement with the Central powers in March 1918. Then civil war broke out in Russia. Rejoining the war in Europe became impossible.

> Why did General Pershing refuse to send his troops into battle right away?
> _____
> _____
> _____

> Why did Russia leave the war?
> _____

WINNING THE WAR

After Russia left the war, Germany decided to move its soldiers from the eastern front to the western front. At the same time, General Pershing sent two divisions of American soldiers to the western front. The fresh troops helped stop

Lesson 3, *continued*

the German advance on Paris. The Americans
had helped bring about one of the major turning
points in the war.

   With more than 1 million American troops in
France, the Allies began attacking German
positions. Soon the Germans were retreating.
Many U.S. soldiers became heroes. One group of
African American soldiers, known as the Harlem
Hellfighters, received the Cross of War medal
from France for their bravery.

   By November 1918 U.S. and Allied soldiers
were moving quickly toward Germany. The Allies
were also winning the war at sea. They used a
new strategy, the convoy system, to protect
merchant ships from the U-boats. Destroyers
capable of sinking U-boats protected groups of
Allied merchant ships.

**What new strategy helped
protect merchant ships
from German attacks?**

_____

ARMISTICE

Germans were tired of the war. Food was scarce.
The country was running out of soldiers.
Germany's allies were also ready to end the war.
Several of them signed peace agreements and
stopped fighting. On November 4 the German
leader, Kaiser Wilhelm II, gave up his throne and
left Germany.

   The Germans agreed to a ceasefire. The Allies
demanded that Germany return all conquered
territory and destroy its weapons. The Germans
accepted the demands. An **armistice** went into
effect on November 11, 1918.

**What did the Allies demand
that Germany do as part of
its surrender?**

_____

_____

CHALLENGE ACTIVITY

Critical Thinking: Make Inferences Imagine that
you are an Allied leader at the end of World
War I. Why would you want Germany to destroy
all of its weapons as part of a peace treaty?

Guided Reading Workbook

DIRECTIONS Read each sentence and fill in the blank with the word in the word pair that best completes the sentence.

1. In 1917 Russia was taken over by _____. (the American Expeditionary Force/Communists)

2. The _____ arrived in Europe in early 1918 and assisted the British and French armies. (American Expeditionary Force/ armistice)

3. The _____ ended the war between the Central and Allied powers. (armistice/Communists)

DIRECTIONS Write two phrases that describe each term below. Include details from the lesson.

4. American Expeditionary Force _____

_____

5. Communists _____

_____

6. armistice _____

_____

DIRECTIONS Match the terms in the first column with their correct definitions from the second column by placing the letter of the correct definition in the space provided before each term.

_____ 7. American Expeditionary Force

_____ 8. Communists

_____ 9. armistice

a. fought for the equal distribution of wealth

b. fought as an independent group instead of merging with French and British troops

c. the truce that ended the war

> **MAIN IDEAS**
> 1. The costs of war included millions of human lives as well as financial burdens.
> 2. President Woodrow Wilson and European leaders met to work out a peace agreement.
> 3. The U.S. Senate rejected the Treaty of Versailles.

Key Terms and People

League of Nations international assembly of nations to settle disputes among countries and encourage democracy

reparations payments for war damages

Treaty of Versailles final peace settlement of World War I

Henry Cabot Lodge senator who led Republican opposition to the ratification of the Treaty of Versailles

Lesson Summary
THE COSTS OF WAR

More lives were lost in World War I than in any previous war. More than 8 million soldiers died and more than 20 million were wounded. The war also caused financial ruin and led to food shortages in much of Europe.

In 1918 a flu epidemic spread across the world. The disease spread rapidly, changing life in many places. The flu killed more people than had died in the war. By 1919 more than 800,000 Americans had died from the flu.

> Underline the number of soldiers killed and wounded in World War I.

> What disease killed more people than had died in the war?
> _____
> _____

THE PEACE AGREEMENT

President Woodrow Wilson had a vision for the postwar world. His plan for peace became known as the Fourteen Points, and the plan included ways to settle border questions. It encouraged military cutbacks, lower trade tariffs, and a ban on secret agreements between nations. The final point in Wilson's plan called for the creation of the **League of Nations**, whose mission would be

> What was the final point of Wilson's Fourteen Points?
> _____
> _____

to settle disputes among countries and to promote democracy. In this way, people would be allowed to choose their own government.

Some Allied leaders disagreed with Wilson's plan. They wanted to punish Germany. They also wanted to make sure Germany could never again become a world power. Leaders from the United States, Britain, France, and Italy met at a peace conference to discuss the terms. Many leaders insisted on **reparations**, which were set at $33 billion.

Wilson reluctantly agreed to the **Treaty of Versailles** (ver-SY). The League of Nations was formed, and the map of Europe was reshaped. Several new and independent countries were formed.

TREATY OF VERSAILLES REJECTED

In the United States, treaties must be ratified by at least two-thirds of the Senate. Republican senators, led by **Henry Cabot Lodge**, insisted on changes to the treaty before ratifying it. They were afraid that the League of Nations could force the United States to send American troops to war.

Wilson refused to compromise. He worked to get the treaty ratified exactly as it was written. On November 1, 1919, a vote to ratify the Treaty of Versailles failed in the Senate. Wilson was extremely disappointed. The United States signed separate peace treaties with the Central powers and did not join the League of Nations.

> **Why did some senators object to the Treaty of Versailles?**
> _____
> _____

CHALLENGE ACTIVITY

Critical Thinking: Explain Imagine that you are a senator in 1919. Write a paragraph explaining why you support or oppose the Treaty of Versailles.

| Henry Cabot Lodge | reparations |
| League of Nations | Treaty of Versailles |

DIRECTIONS Read each sentence and choose the correct term from the word bank to replace the underlined word or phrase. Write the term in the space provided and then define the term in your own words.

1. This agreement included the establishment of the League of Nations and reshaped the map of Europe. _____

   Your definition: _____

   _____

2. President Wilson hoped that this organization would lead to peace in the future. _____

   Your definition: _____

   _____

3. This statesman worked hard to stop the ratification of the Treaty of Versailles. _____

   Your definition: _____

   _____

4. Germany was forced to pay this and to accept blame for the war. _____

   Your definition: _____

   _____

MAIN IDEAS
1. President Harding promised a return to peace and prosperity.
2. Calvin Coolidge supported a probusiness agenda.
3. American business boomed in the 1920s.
4. In 1928 Americans elected Herbert Hoover, hoping he would help good financial times continue.

Key Terms and People

Warren G. Harding Republican president from Ohio elected in 1920

Calvin Coolidge became president when Harding died; reelected to office in 1924

Teapot Dome scandal the acceptance of bribes by Secretary of the Interior Albert Fall in exchange for control of government oil reserves

Kellogg-Briand Pact an unenforceable agreement among 62 nations to outlaw war

Model T a low-cost automobile invented by Ford

moving assembly line production system that moves parts between groups of workers

Herbert Hoover president elected in 1928 with promises for more prosperity

Lesson Summary
RETURN TO PEACE AND PROSPERITY

As the war ended, millions of soldiers came home. However, factories had stopped making war supplies, so many people could not find jobs. But demand for goods was high, so prices rose. People who did have jobs, though, couldn't afford the goods, so many went on strike for higher wages.

Warren G. Harding ran for president with running mate **Calvin Coolidge**. Harding promised a return to "normalcy." After he was elected, Harding worked hard to strengthen the economy. He used tax cuts for the wealthy as an incentive to invest in business. As a result, an economic boom started.

What was Warren G. Harding's campaign promise?

_____

Harding's term in office was filled with problems outside the economy. Several appointees used their power to get wealthy by illegal means. In the worst scandal, Secretary of the Interior Albert Fall accepted large amounts of money and gifts from private oil companies and allowed the companies to control government oil reserves. He was convicted of taking bribes, and the scandal became known as the **Teapot Dome scandal**.

> **Why did the Teapot Dome scandal reflect badly on President Harding?**
>
> _____
>
> _____

COOLIDGE'S PROBUSINESS ADMINISTRATION

When Harding died in 1923, Vice-President Coolidge became president. He acted quickly to clean up the government. He was more probusiness than Harding. He pushed tax cuts and higher tariffs. During his term, the United States and 14 other nations signed the **Kellogg-Briand Pact**. However, there was no way to enforce the effort to ban war.

> **How did Coolidge's policies differ from Harding's?**
>
> _____
>
> _____

BUSINESS BOOMS

In the 1920s U.S. business boomed as factories changed. Henry Ford built the **Model T**, a car many people could afford. He reduced costs using a **moving assembly line**. Ford raised wages and reduced the workday to eight hours. He also hired workers that other factories would not hire, such as African Americans and people with disabilities.

Millions found jobs in the automobile industry. Travel increased, spurring business. Companies produced goods that took advantage of the increasing number of homes with electricity.

> **Circle the name of the first automobile that the general public could afford.**

HOOVER ELECTED

In 1928 Secretary of Commerce **Herbert Hoover** ran for president with promises to continue the prosperity. He easily defeated Al Smith, whose campaign focused on city dwellers. For many voters, Smith's religious faith also was an issue.

> **Why would voters most likely have elected Herbert Hoover?**
>
> _____
>
> _____
>
> _____

CHALLENGE ACTIVITY

Critical Thinking: Hypothesize The availability of electricity in homes was an economic boost. Write a paragraph about how things might have been different in the 1920s without electricity.

DIRECTIONS Look at each set of terms below. On the line provided, write the letter of the term that does not relate to the others.

_____ 1. a. Warren G. Harding
       b. Calvin Coolidge
       c. Henry Ford
       d. Herbert Hoover

_____ 2. a. Kellogg-Briand Pact
       b. Teapot Dome scandal
       c. corruption
       d. Warren G. Harding

_____ 3. a. moving assembly line
       b. Henry Ford
       c. Calvin Coolidge
       d. Model T

_____ 4. a. Calvin Coolidge
       b. Kellogg-Briand Pact
       c. war
       d. Herbert Hoover

_____ 5. a. Henry Ford
       b. Warren G. Harding
       c. Model T
       d. affordable

DIRECTIONS On the line provided before each statement, write **T** if a statement is true and **F** if a statement is false. If the statement is false, write the correct term on the line after each sentence that makes the sentence a true statement.

_____ 6. The Kellogg-Briand Pact involved bribes paid by private oil companies to government officials.

_____

_____ 7. Henry Ford used an assembly line in his factories to speed production.

_____

_____ 8. Calvin Coolidge was more probusiness than Warren G. Harding had been.

_____

_____ 9. The Model T was the first affordable automobile.

_____

_____10. <u>Herbert Hoover</u> promised limited government spending and a return to "normalcy."

_____

The Roaring Twenties

Lesson 2

MAIN IDEAS

1. In the 1920s many young people found new independence in a changing society.
2. Postwar tensions occasionally led to fear and violence.
3. Competing ideals caused conflict between Americans with traditional beliefs and those with modern views.
4. Following the war, minority groups organized to demand their civil rights.

Key Terms and People

flappers young women in the 1920s who challenged traditional women's roles

Red Scare period of fear of Communists and radicals in the United States

Twenty-First Amendment constitutional amendment that repealed prohibition

fundamentalism belief in a word-for-word interpretation of the Bible

Scopes trial the trial of John Scopes for teaching evolution in school

Great Migration the movement of African Americans to northern cities

Marcus Garvey black leader who encouraged black people to express pride in their culture

Lesson Summary

A CHANGING SOCIETY

World War I changed the way people saw the world. People moved to cities, and for the first time, more Americans lived in cities than in rural areas.

Young adults had more personal freedom than in the past, and they were better educated. Also, more women had joined the workforce, and they had new opportunities. **Flappers** challenged the traditional ideas of how women should behave.

> How did World War I change society in the 1920s?
>
> _____
>
> _____

FEAR AND VIOLENCE

Some of the social changes of the 1920s were violent. There were massive labor strikes caused by unemployment and inflation. As Communists took control in Russia, the **Red Scare** led to action against Communists in the United States.

Some people saw immigrants as a threat to their jobs and culture, which led to a fear of foreigners. Laws were passed to restrict the number of immigrants. The Emergency Quota Act of 1921 gave preference to immigrants from western Europe. A 1924 law banned immigration from East Asia.

> **Why were some Americans afraid of immigration to the United States?**
> _____
> _____

COMPETING IDEALS

Differences were also growing between older rural traditions and modern urban society. One issue was prohibition, which was hard to enforce. It led to corruption and created new ways for criminals to get rich. In 1933 prohibition was ended by the **Twenty-First Amendment** to the Constitution.

> **Circle the name of the act that marked the end of prohibition in the United States.**

Religious leaders saw a move away from traditional values. In response, **fundamentalism** grew strong in rural areas. The fundamentalists believed in an exact, word-for-word reading of the Bible. They believed that scientific theories such as evolution contradicted the Bible. The **Scopes trial** was the center of a national debate over modern science and religious values.

MINORITY RIGHTS

The **Great Migration** continued during the economic boom of the 1920s. Economic recession led to racial tensions in many cities. Minorities, including African Americans and Hispanic Americans, began fighting to protect their rights. **Marcus Garvey** encouraged pride in black culture. Native Americans gained the rights of citizenship and fought to protect their lands.

> **Why do you think the Great Migration continued even after World War I ended?**
> _____
> _____
> _____

CHALLENGE ACTIVITY

Critical Thinking: Compare Write a paragraph comparing immigration issues today with immigration issues in the 1920s.

DIRECTIONS Read each sentence and fill in the blank with the word in the word pair that best completes the sentence.

1. A time of fear of Communists was known as _____. (fundamentalism/the Red Scare)

2. The failed experiment of prohibition was officially ended with the _____. (Scopes trial/Twenty-First Amendment)

3. _____ challenged the traditional roles of women in the 1920s. (Flappers/Fundamentalism)

4. _____ encouraged black people around the world to express pride in their culture. (Fundamentalism/Marcus Garvey)

5. Large numbers of African Americans moved to the North searching for factory jobs as part of the _____. (Great Migration/Red Scare)

DIRECTIONS Match the terms in the first column with their correct definitions from the second column by placing the letter of the correct definition in the space provided before each term.

_____ 6. Red Scare

_____ 7. flappers

_____ 8. Scopes trial

_____ 9. fundamentalism

_____ 10. Marcus Garvey

a. belief in a word-for-word interpretation of the Bible

b. encouraged pride in black culture

c. led to actions against many suspected Communists and radicals

d. a legal fight over the teaching of evolution

e. openly challenged ideas of how women were supposed to behave

MAIN IDEAS
1. Radio and movies linked the country in a national culture.
2. Jazz and blues music became popular nationwide.
3. Writers and artists introduced new styles and artistic ideas.

Key Terms and People

talkie motion picture with sound

Jazz Age name given to the 1920s due to the popularity of jazz music

Harlem Renaissance period of African American artistic accomplishment in New York City

Langston Hughes poet and writer who wrote about African American life

Lost Generation writers in the 1920s who criticized American society

expatriates people who live outside their home country

Georgia O'Keeffe innovative artist famous for her detailed drawings of flowers

Lesson Summary
A NATIONAL CULTURE

The radio helped build a new national culture during the 1920s. People from around the country were able to share common experiences. Radio networks broadcast the same programs to hundreds of stations at a time.

> How did radio change the ability of people to share experiences?
>
> _____
> _____
> _____

Movies also opened up a new, exciting means of entertainment and adventure. Fans were thrilled by the first movie with sound, or **talkie**. The first talkie, *The Jazz Singer*, premiered in 1927. Movie stars became heroes to millions of Americans.

> Circle the name of the first talkie.

Other people became heroes as well. Fans packed baseball stadiums and other athletic events. George Herman "Babe" Ruth broke home-run records. He brought many new fans to the sport of baseball. Pilots, such as Charles Lindbergh and Amelia Earhart, became nationally known as they broke flight records.

New ideas such as psychoanalysis entered popular culture.

POPULAR MUSIC

The booming economy and new forms of entertainment caused the decade to be named the Roaring Twenties. Another nickname was the **Jazz Age** because jazz music became so popular.

Jazz developed in New Orleans as a blend of African American spirituals, European harmonies, and West African rhythms. One famous jazz musician, Louis Armstrong, was known for stepping out from the band to play a solo on his trumpet. African Americans brought this music north during the Great Migration. Blues music was born in the rural South during slavery and became popular in the 1920s. Both jazz and the blues were musical innovations that remain popular today.

> What kinds of music were the sources of jazz music?
> _____
> _____
> _____

> In what segment of the American population did many of the music innovations of the 1920s originate?
> _____

WRITERS AND ARTISTS

Writers and artists also changed American culture. The **Harlem Renaissance** included writers **Langston Hughes** and Claude McKay. They told of African American life in stories, poems, and plays. Zora Neale Hurston's writings told of the experiences of African American women.

Many American writers told of their experiences in the United States and around the world. Young writers of the **Lost Generation** expressed feelings of separation from American society. Some formed a community of **expatriates** in Paris. Lost Generation writers included Ernest Hemingway, F. Scott Fitzgerald, and Sinclair Lewis. Lewis became the first American to win the Nobel Prize in literature.

Painters like **Georgia O'Keeffe** experimented with new styles and ways to express themselves. Meanwhile, architects were designing skyscrapers that still define American city skylines today.

> Why would many writers of the Lost Generation become expatriates?
> _____
> _____

CHALLENGE ACTIVITY

Critical Thinking: Elaborate Imagine that you have just moved to a city in the 1920s. Write a short letter to a friend telling how life in the city is different from rural life.

expatriates	Jazz Age	Lost Generation
Georgia O'Keeffe	Langston Hughes	talkies
Harlem Renaissance		

DIRECTIONS Use the seven terms from the word bank to write a summary of what you learned in the lesson.

_____

_____

_____

_____

_____

_____

_____

DIRECTIONS Look at each set of terms below. On the line provided, write the letter of the term that does not relate to the others.

_____ 1. a. Lost Generation
      b. expatriates
      c. talkie
      d. Ernest Hemingway

_____ 2. a. F. Scott Fitzgerald
      b. Harlem Renaissance
      c. Zora Neale Hurston
      d. Langston Hughes

_____ 3. a. Jazz Age
      b. Harlem Renaissance
      c. Lost Generation
      d. Charles Lindbergh

_____ 4. a. Georgia O'Keeffe
      b. George Herman "Babe" Ruth
      c. Langston Hughes
      d. Louis Armstrong

Name _____ Class _____ Date _____

The Great Depression

Lesson 1

MAIN IDEAS
1. The U.S. stock market crashed in 1929.
2. The economy collapsed after the stock market crash.
3. Many Americans were dissatisfied with Hoover's reaction to economic conditions.
4. Roosevelt defeated Hoover in the election of 1932.

Key Terms and People

buying on margin purchasing stocks on credit, or with borrowed money

Black Tuesday Tuesday, October 29, 1929, the day of the stock market crash

business cycle up-and-down pattern of business production and unemployment

Great Depression severe economic depression that followed the stock market crash of 1929

Bonus Army unemployed World War I veterans who camped in a new Hooverville in Washington, DC, to demand early payment of military bonuses

Franklin D. Roosevelt New York governor elected president in the 1932 election

Lesson Summary

THE STOCK MARKET CRASHES

During the 1920s stock prices rose rapidly. Many people bought stocks by **buying on margin**, hoping to sell them later at a large profit. In 1929 stock prices began to drop. Frightened investors sold stocks to pay off their loans, but there were few buyers. On October 29, known as **Black Tuesday**, the stock market crashed. Investors lost everything.

THE ECONOMY COLLAPSES

The stock market crash caused a banking crisis as banks lost their investments. People tried to withdraw all of their money and many banks went out of business. This crisis contributed to losses by businesses, which then needed fewer

Why did many banks go out of business after the stock market crash?

_____

_____

© Houghton Mifflin Harcourt Publishing Company

Guided Reading Workbook

Lesson 1, *continued*

workers. Normally when businesses produce more than they can sell, they have to cut back production. As people are laid off, the demand for goods drops. This can cause a severe recession called a depression. When the economy bounces back, more people are hired, and demand increases. This pattern of ups and downs in the economy is called a **business cycle**.

> **What normally happens in the business cycle after a recession?**
> _____
> _____

The economy was slow to recover after the crash in 1929. This period, the **Great Depression**, had several causes. One was overproduction of goods as the market was shrinking. Other factors were the uneven division of wealth and limited world trade.

HOOVER'S REACTION

President Hoover knew that people needed help. He did not believe, however, that it was the role of the federal government to provide direct relief. He did implement some new programs to help banks and other institutions recover. This did little to help the economy and left many people homeless. They built shacks in cities and towns called Hoovervilles.

> **Underline the sentence that explains why President Hoover did not implement relief programs to help people who were struggling.**

In 1932 the **Bonus Army** built a Hooverville in Washington, DC. These veterans wanted early payment of military bonuses. Hoover sent U.S. troops to evict them, and when several people were killed, the public was outraged.

ELECTION OF 1932

The Republican Party nominated Herbert Hoover again in 1932. However, many people blamed him for the Great Depression. The Democratic nominee was **Franklin D. Roosevelt**. As governor, he had worked to provide aid to citizens of New York. In particular, he had provided aid to farmers. Roosevelt promised a "new deal" for the American people, and he won the election in a landslide.

> **Why did people believe Roosevelt would keep his promise to provide aid?**
> _____
> _____
> _____

Guided Reading Workbook

Lesson 1, *continued*

CHALLENGE ACTIVITY

Critical Thinking: Make Judgments Do you think
the American people were justified in blaming
Herbert Hoover for the Great Depression? Write
a paragraph to explain your position.

Black Tuesday	business cycle	Franklin D. Roosevelt
Bonus Army	buying on margin	Great Depression

DIRECTIONS On the line provided before each statement, write **T** if
a statement is true and **F** if a statement is false. If the statement is
false, write the correct term or name on the line after each sentence
that makes the sentence a true statement.

_____ 1. The up-and-down pattern of the economy is known as the Great
Depression.

_____

_____ 2. When an investor bought stocks with borrowed money, that person
was buying on margin.

_____

_____ 3. In contrast to Herbert Hoover, the Bonus Army promised to provide
aid to Americans who were suffering from the Great Depression.

_____

_____ 4. The stock market crash on October 29, 1929, became known as the
business cycle.

_____

_____ 5. The economic downturn following the stock market crash in 1929 was
called the Great Depression because of its severity and length.

_____

_____ 6. The Bonus Army lived in a Hooverville in Washington, DC.

_____

The Great Depression

MAIN IDEAS
1. Congress approved many new programs during the Hundred Days.
2. Critics expressed concerns about the New Deal.
3. New Deal programs continued through Roosevelt's first term in what became known as the Second New Deal.
4. Roosevelt clashed with the Supreme Court over the New Deal.

Key Terms and People

New Deal programs developed by Roosevelt to aid economic recovery

fireside chats radio addresses in which Roosevelt spoke directly to the public

Tennessee Valley Authority New Deal program to build dams and generators to provide electricity in the Tennessee River valley

Frances Perkins Roosevelt's Secretary of Labor, the nation's first female cabinet member

Eleanor Roosevelt First Lady in the Roosevelt administration; supported the New Deal

Social Security Act federal law that started programs to ensure economic well-being of citizens who could not provide for themselves

Congress of Industrial Organizations new union that organized workers based on industry, not skill level

sit-down strike strategy in which striking workers remained inside the workplace

Lesson Summary
THE HUNDRED DAYS

Roosevelt told Americans that economic recovery was possible. He called Congress into a special session, known as the Hundred Days. They created the **New Deal** to aid economic recovery.

One program was the Emergency Banking Relief Act. It was passed to restore confidence in banks. The president talked about it in his first **fireside chat**.

Other programs such as the Civil Works Administration (CWA) put people to work on public projects, such as roads, airports, and

> **Why was the Emergency Banking Relief Act passed?**
> _____
> _____

Guided Reading Workbook

parks. The **Tennessee Valley Authority** (TVA) hired people to build dams to provide electricity to poor communities. **Frances Perkins** helped pass the National Industrial Recovery Act to assist businesses.

NEW DEAL CRITICS

Critics of the New Deal felt it went too far or not far enough. The American Liberty League, for example, disliked the expansion of the federal government and the authority of the president. Others thought there should be higher taxes for the rich and guaranteed income for the poor.

> **What were the criticisms of the New Deal?**
> _____
> _____
> _____

THE NEW DEAL CONTINUES

The Second New Deal was introduced in 1934. The Works Progress Administration (WPA) employed more than 8.5 million people. **Eleanor Roosevelt** supported programs for young people. Congress passed the **Social Security Act** to help children and the elderly, disabled, and unemployed.

The New Deal included new labor laws. The **Congress of Industrial Organizations** (CIO) was a union based on industry. It welcomed women, immigrants, and minority groups. The CIO used a **sit-down strike** to keep General Motors from replacing strikers. Workers stayed in the factories. This success helped the unions grow stronger.

> **Why would a sit-down strike be more effective than just staying home?**
> _____
> _____

CLASHES WITH THE COURT

Democrats controlled the presidency and the Congress but not the Supreme Court. The Supreme Court declared several New Deal programs unconstitutional. Roosevelt's plan to increase the number of justices was defeated in Congress.

CHALLENGE ACTIVITY

Critical Thinking: Analyze Research one of the
New Deal programs. Write a three-paragraph
report about its effects.

DIRECTIONS Look at each set of terms and names below. On the
line provided, write the letter of the term or name that does not
relate to the others.

_____ 1. a. New Deal
b. Social Security Act
c. sit-down strike
d. Tennessee Valley Authority

_____ 2. a. Congress of Industrial
Organizations
b. Frances Perkins
c. Civil Works Administration
d. Franklin D. Roosevelt

_____ 3. a. sit-down strike
b. labor laws
c. Social Security Act
d. Congress of Industrial Organizations

_____ 4. a. New Deal
b. Franklin D. Roosevelt
c. fireside chat
d. American Liberty
League

_____ 5. a. Supreme Court
b. Social Security Act
c. Civil Works
Administration
d. Tennessee Valley
Authority

DIRECTIONS Match the terms in the first column with their correct
definitions from the second column by placing the letter of the
correct definition in the space provided before each term.

_____ 6. New Deal

_____ 7. Tennessee Valley Authority

_____ 8. Social Security Act

_____ 9. Congress of Industrial
Organizations

_____ 10. sit-down strike

a. brought electricity and jobs to
many poor communities

b. workers stayed in a factory so
they could not be replaced by
new workers

c. provided basic economic security
for the elderly and disabled

d. the system of government
programs meant to improve the
economy

e. a new union based on industry,
not on skill level

The Great Depression

MAIN IDEAS
1. Parts of the Great Plains came to be known as the Dust Bowl as severe drought destroyed farms there.
2. Families all over the United States faced hard times.
3. Depression-era culture helped lift people's spirits.
4. The New Deal had lasting effects on American society.

Key Terms and People

Dust Bowl region of the Great Plains affected by extreme drought and dust storms

Mary McLeod Bethune African American educator appointed as an adviser by President Roosevelt

John Steinbeck novelist who wrote about the hardships of the Great Depression in *The Grapes of Wrath*

Woody Guthrie Depression-era folksinger from Oklahoma

Lesson Summary
THE DUST BOWL

American farmers were already having difficult times before the Great Depression, but then the situation got worse. In the early 1930s a severe drought hit the Great Plains. In the **Dust Bowl** region, topsoil blew away, and farmers could not grow crops. Many could not pay their mortgages, so they lost their farms.

Although several New Deal programs tried to help farmers, they came too late for most. About 2.5 million people left the Great Plains. Many of them drove to California to look for jobs. They often found that there were already too many workers. Eventually, soil conservation programs were created to help prevent another Dust Bowl.

> **Why did so many farmers move from the Great Plains to California during the Dust Bowl period?**
>
> _____
> _____
> _____

HARD TIMES

During the Great Depression, many families had to split up as people looked for work in different places. Children dropped out of school to help support their families.

The Great Depression was especially hard on minority groups. Many faced discrimination and lost jobs to unemployed white workers. But some found jobs through relief programs. Several African American leaders, including educator **Mary McLeod Bethune**, advised the president. They became known as the Black Cabinet.

> **What was the Black Cabinet?**
> _____
> _____

Eleanor Roosevelt was a strong advocate of equal rights. She resigned from the Daughters of the American Revolution when they refused to rent a hall to African American singer Marian Anderson.

DEPRESSION-ERA CULTURE

In 1935 the Works Progress Administration put many artists, writers, and actors to work. Musicians went to rural areas to record traditional music. They preserved culture that might have been lost. Writers interviewed Americans from different backgrounds. They kept a record of their lives and memories.

> **Underline the name of the New Deal program that helped artists, writers, and musicians.**

John Steinbeck was deeply affected by the hardships of the Depression. He wrote novels about Depression life. Folksinger **Woody Guthrie** crossed the country, writing and singing songs of loss and struggle. At the same time, swing music became popular because it helped people forget about their troubles. Movies were yet another form of escape.

> **Why were lively music and movies so popular during the Great Depression?**
> _____
> _____

EFFECTS OF THE NEW DEAL

People still disagree about the New Deal's effects. Critics argue that recovery did not occur until the U.S. entered World War II. Supporters say it gave Americans hope during a crisis. It did expand the role of the federal government, and some of its programs, such as Social Security and the Federal Deposit Insurance Corporation, remain important.

> **Circle the names of two New Deal programs that still exist today.**

CHALLENGE ACTIVITY

Critical Thinking: Make Inferences Imagine what it would be like to grow up during the Great Depression. Write a short poem about what your life might have been like.

Dust Bowl	Mary McLeod Bethune
John Steinbeck	Woody Guthrie

DIRECTIONS Use the four terms or names from the word list to write a summary of what you learned in this lesson.

_____

_____

_____

_____

_____

_____

DIRECTIONS Read each sentence and fill in the blank with the word in the word pair that best completes the sentence.

1. _____ was a famous American novelist who wrote about average Americans during the Great Depression. (John Steinbeck/ Woody Guthrie)

2. _____ was an African American adviser to President Roosevelt. (Woody Guthrie/Mary McLeod Bethune)

3. Because of _____, soil conservation programs were established to help preserve farmland. (Mary McLeod Bethune/the Dust Bowl)

4. _____ was a folksinger who wrote songs about people's struggles during the Great Depression. (Woody Guthrie/Mary McLeod Bethune)

World War II

MAIN IDEAS
1. During the 1930s, totalitarian governments rose to power in Europe and Japan.
2. German expansion led to the start of World War II in Europe in 1939.
3. The United States joined the war after Japan attacked Pearl Harbor in 1941.

Key Terms and People

totalitarianism political system in which the government controls every aspect of citizens' lives

Benito Mussolini fascist Italian dictator who ruled from 1922 to 1943

fascism political system in which the government is seen as more important than individuals

Adolf Hitler politician and World War I veteran who took advantage of public anger to become chancellor of Germany in 1933

Nazis National Socialist Party members; controlled Germany from 1933 to 1945

Joseph Stalin Communist dictator of the Soviet Union who gained control in 1928

Axis powers World War II alliance of Germany, Italy, and Japan

appeasement policy of avoiding war by giving in to demands

Winston Churchill British prime minister during World War II

Allied powers alliance between Great Britain and France in 1939, and later, the Soviet Union and the United States

Lend-Lease Act law allowing the president to aid any nation vital to U.S. defense

Pearl Harbor U.S. naval base in Hawaii attacked by Japan on December 7, 1941

Lesson Summary
THE RISE OF TOTALITARIANISM

The 1930s were hard times. Many people were willing to give up rights to leaders who promised them a better future. In Europe and Asia, some countries moved toward **totalitarianism**.

> Why did totalitarian leaders gain support in Europe and Asia after World War I?
>
> _____
>
> _____

Benito Mussolini took control of Italy in 1922. Under **fascism**, Mussolini restored order and improved the economy.

In Germany **Adolf Hitler** used anger over World War I to gain power. His **Nazis** took control in 1933.

Joseph Stalin became dictator of the Soviet Union in 1929. Stalin ruled by fear and scare tactics. He killed or jailed millions.

In Japan military leaders slowly took over the government. Then in 1931 Japan invaded northern China.

GERMANY EXPANDS

Hitler rebuilt the military in Germany. His goal was to start a new empire. In 1936 Germany joined Italy and Japan to form the **Axis powers**. Hitler took over part of Czechoslovakia in 1938. Although Britain and France were allied with Czechoslovakia, they chose **appeasement**. But British admiral Winston Churchill warned that the policy would fail.

In 1939 Germany and the Soviet Union made a secret pact to split Poland between them. Germany attacked Poland and won, starting World War II. The **Allied powers** declared war on Germany.

In 1940 Germany conquered much of Europe, including France. Britain stood alone. With new radar technology, the British Royal Air Force was able to stop an invasion of Britain.

> **What countries were included in the Axis powers?**
> _____
> _____

> **Underline the name of the new technology that helped the British prevent a German invasion.**

THE UNITED STATES JOINS THE WAR

Most Americans wanted to stay out of the war in Europe. In 1941 the **Lend-Lease Act** was passed to allow the president to aid any nation vital to U.S. defense. The United States began sending supplies to Britain and other Allied countries.

The United States also decided to act against Japanese imperialism. This angered Japan. On December 7, 1941, Japan attacked the naval fleet at **Pearl Harbor** in Hawaii. The United States declared war on Japan. Then Germany declared war on the United States. The United States joined the Allies, entering another world war.

> **Why did the United States enter World War II?**
> _____
> _____

CHALLENGE ACTIVITY

Critical Thinking: Make Judgments Explain why you believe that the United States should or should not have helped the Allies through the Lend-Lease Act.

Adolf Hitler	Axis powers	Joseph Stalin	Pearl Harbor
Allied powers	Benito Mussolini	Lend-Lease Act	Winston Churchill
appeasement	fascism	Nazis	

DIRECTIONS Answer each question by writing a sentence that contains at least one word from the word bank.

1. Who maintained control of the Soviet Union by killing or jailing millions?

   _____

   _____

2. What alliance fought Britain and the United States in World War II?

   _____

   _____

3. Who used anger over what happened after World War I to gain power in Germany?

   _____

   _____

4. What law provided aid to nations vital to the defense of the United States before the United States had entered the war?

_____

_____

5. Under what political system is the government seen as more important than individuals?

_____

_____

Lesson 2

MAIN IDEAS
1. Businesses, soldiers, and citizens worked to prepare the United States for war.
2. The war brought new opportunities for many women and minorities.
3. Japanese Americans faced internment during the war.

Key Terms and People

War Production Board agency that converted factories for war production

A. Philip Randolph African American labor leader

Tuskegee Airmen African American pilots who trained in Tuskegee, Alabama

Benjamin O. Davis Jr. group leader of Tuskegee Airmen and later the first African American general in the U.S. Air Force

zoot-suit riots Los Angeles riots in which white mobs attacked Mexican Americans

internment imprisonment of Japanese Americans during World War II

Lesson Summary
DOMINANCE OF BIG BUSINESS

The Great Depression finally ended as the United States mobilized for war. The **War Production Board** was created. The Selective Training and Service Act started the first peacetime draft in the history of the United States. More than 16 million Americans served in World War II.

To fund the war, the government raised taxes and sold war bonds. Americans also gathered scrap metal for war production factories. Government rations curbed the nonmilitary use of gasoline, rubber, shoes, and some kinds of food.

> Circle the number of Americans who served in World War II.

WARTIME OPPORTUNITIES

Women took on a new role in World War II. Because so many men left to fight in the war, women were urged to fill factory jobs. Women also served in the armed forces, some as pilots

> Why did women take factory jobs during the war?
>
> _____
>
> _____
>
> _____

and as nurses. Over 300,000 women served in the armed forces during World War II.

The Great Migration continued as African Americans moved north to find factory jobs supporting the war effort. A march was planned by **A. Philip Randolph** to protest lower wages for African Americans. It was called off when Roosevelt ended the practice of racial discrimination in factories that produced war goods.

About 1 million African Americans served in the armed forces during the war. Most of them were sent to support jobs in segregated units. The **Tuskegee Airmen**, under the leadership of **Benjamin O. Davis Jr.**, flew thousands of successful missions in North Africa and Italy.

About 300,000 Mexican Americans served in the military during the war. Many also found wartime jobs in the West and Midwest. Mexico supplied farm workers to ease a lack in the United States. Despite their aiding the war effort, Mexican Americans faced discrimination. In Los Angeles in June 1943, groups of sailors attacked Mexican Americans wearing zoot suits. Zoot suits were fancy, loose-fitting outfits with oversized hats. This started the **zoot-suit riots**.

Explain how World War II helped some African Americans.
_____
_____
_____

Underline the name of the African American unit of pilots who flew in World War II.

JAPANESE AMERICAN INTERNMENT

After the attack on Pearl Harbor, fear of Japanese Americans on the West Coast increased. No evidence to back up the fear was offered, but the government began the process of **internment** of Japanese Americans. About 120,000 people, many of them native-born Americans, were forced to move and were held in internment camps. Many lost their jobs, homes, and belongings.

After Pearl Harbor, Japanese Americans could not join the military. This policy ended in 1943.

When were Japanese Americans moved to internment camps?
_____
_____

About 33,000 Japanese Americans served in segregated units in World War II.

CHALLENGE ACTIVITY

Critical Thinking: Analyze What assumptions did the U.S. government make about Japanese Americans when it moved them to internment camps?

DIRECTIONS In the space provided, write the letter of the description that best matches each term or person.

_____ 1. War Production Board

_____ 2. A. Philip Randolph

_____ 3. Tuskegee Airmen

_____ 4. Benjamin O. Davis Jr.

_____ 5. zoot-suit riots

_____ 6. internment

a. group of African American pilots trained in Alabama

b. attacks by white mobs against Mexican Americans

c. agency that oversaw the conversion of factories for war production

d. first African American general in the U.S. Air Force

e. labor leader who organized a protest over lower wages for African Americans

f. imprisonment of Japanese Americans during World War II

DIRECTIONS Write two adjectives or descriptive phrases that describe the term.

7. War Production Board _____

_____

8. A. Philip Randolph _____

_____

9. Tuskegee Airmen _____

_____

10. Benjamin O. Davis Jr. _____

_____

11. zoot-suit riots _____

_____

12. internment _____

_____

Lesson 3

MAIN IDEAS
1. The Allies fought back against the Axis powers in North Africa and Europe.
2. Key Allied victories halted the German advance.
3. In the D-Day invasion, Allied forces attacked German-controlled France.

Key Terms and People

Battle of El Alamein battle in which Montgomery's British troops stopped Rommel's *Afrika Korps* in North Africa in November 1942

Dwight D. Eisenhower American general who commanded Allied forces in Europe; later elected U.S. president

Battle of Stalingrad key battle in which Soviets stopped German advance in winter of 1943

D-Day date of Allied sea invasion of occupied France—June 6, 1944

Lesson Summary

THE ALLIES FIGHT BACK

When the United States entered the war, President Roosevelt met with British prime minister Winston Churchill. They decided to attack German forces in North Africa before an invasion of Europe. This angered the Soviet Union, which had been hoping for help on the eastern front.

New technology helped in the effort. Long-range planes dropped bombs on German factories, railroads, and cities. Sonar detected German U-boats.

> **What decision caused the Soviet Union to be angry with the Allies after the United States entered the war?**
>
> _____
> _____
> _____

HALTING THE GERMAN ADVANCE

By 1942 the Germans and the British were fighting in North Africa. They were fighting for control of the Suez Canal. The British forces stopped the German attack at the **Battle of El Alamein**. American general **Dwight D. Eisenhower** led U.S. and British troops through

> **Why did the Germans and the British fight in North Africa?**
>
> _____
> _____

Morocco and Algeria. Trapped, the Germans surrendered in May 1943.

After taking control of North Africa, the Allies moved into Europe. They attacked Italy in 1943. Italian leaders removed Mussolini from power and surrendered to the Allies. Germany sent troops to Italy to stop the Allies. German forces were not pushed out of Italy until 1945.

At the same time, German and Soviet troops were fighting on the eastern front in the Soviet Union. Hitler ordered the German troops not to retreat. However, Germany did not send enough supplies or fresh troops. The German forces surrendered due to supply shortages and the harsh winter. The Soviets blocked the German advance at the **Battle of Stalingrad**, a key turning point in the war. More than 1 million Soviet soldiers died and about 800,000 Axis soldiers were killed.

> **Where was the eastern front of World War II in 1943?**
>
> _____

THE D-DAY INVASION

After succeeding in North Africa and Italy, the Allies made plans to move into France. At the time, the Germans controlled France. General Eisenhower was in charge of planning the largest sea-to-land invasion ever attempted. The invasion took place on **D-Day**, named for the "designated day" of the attack—June 6, 1944.

> **Underline the name of the general in charge of the D-Day landing in France.**

More than 156,000 Allied troops landed on five beaches in Normandy, France. The Germans had placed mines and soldiers along the coast to repel the invasion. Although they suffered heavy losses, the Allies took control of all five beaches by the end of D-Day. Then they could begin moving east through France toward Germany.

> **Why did the Allies suffer heavy casualties during the D-Day landing?**
>
> _____
> _____
> _____

CHALLENGE ACTIVITY

Critical Thinking: Make Inferences Imagine that you are an American soldier on D-Day. Write a

short letter home to a friend or family member
telling them what you are thinking.

Battle of El Alamein	D-Day
Battle of Stalingrad	Dwight D. Eisenhower

DIRECTIONS Use the four vocabulary words from the word bank to
write a summary of what you learned in the lesson.

_____

_____

_____

_____

_____

_____

_____

DIRECTIONS Read each sentence and fill in the blank with the
word in the word pair that best completes the sentence.

1. The German army was stopped in North Africa at the
   _____. (Battle of El Alamein/Battle of Stalingrad)

2. During _____, the Allies attacked German forces with
   one of the largest invasion forces ever assembled. (the Battle of Stalingrad/
   D-Day)

3. The German loss at the _____ was a turning point on the
   eastern front. (Battle of El Alamein/Battle of Stalingrad)

World War II

MAIN IDEAS
1. The Japanese continued advancing across the Pacific in 1942.
2. The Allies stopped Japan's advance with key victories over the Japanese navy.
3. The Allies began battling toward Japan.

Key Terms and People

Douglas MacArthur general who commanded U.S. ground troops in the Pacific

Bataan Death March forced march of American and Filipino prisoners on the Bataan Peninsula, during which many died

Chester Nimitz American admiral who commanded U.S. Pacific fleet

Battle of the Coral Sea naval battle in which the American fleet prevented Japanese invasion of Australia

Battle of Midway key Pacific battle in which Japanese navy was severely weakened

island hopping strategy of attacking only key Pacific islands

Battle of Leyte Gulf largest naval battle in history; American navy defeated the Japanese navy to retake the Philippines

kamikaze tactic of purposely crashing piloted planes into enemy ships

Lesson Summary
JAPAN ADVANCES

The attack on Pearl Harbor left the U.S. Pacific fleet weak. As a result the fleet was not able to react immediately to the assault. In the meantime Japan was able to conquer much of Asia and the Pacific. American forces under the command of U.S. General **Douglas MacArthur** could not stop Japan's advance in the Philippines. MacArthur was forced to leave. MacArthur's forces could not stop the Japanese advance. More than 600 Americans and 10,000 Filipinos died in the **Bataan Death March**.

> Why were the Japanese able to conquer much of the Pacific after the attack on Pearl Harbor?
>
> _____
> _____
> _____

KEY ALLIED VICTORIES

The Allies feared a Japanese attack on India, Australia, or the U.S. mainland. American code breakers learned to read the Japanese secret code, and Admiral **Chester Nimitz** found out that Japan planned to attack Australia. His aircraft carriers and fighter planes fought the Japanese in the **Battle of the Coral Sea** and stopped the invasion.

The Allies learned that Japan was planning a surprise attack on the Midway Islands. Nimitz was ready for the attack. The Allies destroyed four Japanese carriers at the **Battle of Midway**, badly weakening the Japanese navy. This allowed U.S. Marines to invade Guadalcanal. Allied forces took full control of the island six months later.

> **What advantage did the American Pacific fleet have over the Japanese?**
> _____
> _____
> _____

BATTLING TOWARD JAPAN

The battles at Midway and Guadalcanal were key victories. This **island hopping** strategy was successful but hard to execute. The Allied forces slowly moved across the Pacific.

In October 1944 General MacArthur led his forces to retake the Philippines. The Allies won the **Battle of Leyte Gulf**. After the battle MacArthur's troops fought for many more months to drive out the remaining Japanese forces.

Allied planes began bombing Japan in November 1944. At this time they fought two of the fiercest battles of the war on the islands of Iwo Jima and Okinawa.

Near Okinawa, Japanese pilots used **kamikaze** tactics against American ships. More than 2,500 kamikaze missions were flown. After the victories at Iwo Jima and Okinawa, the Allies began to plan an assault on the main Japanese islands.

> **What general led the mission to regain control of the Philippines?**
> _____

> **Underline the tactic Japanese pilots used at the Battle of Okinawa.**

CHALLENGE ACTIVITY

Critical Thinking: Make Inferences Why was
island hopping a difficult strategy to execute?

DIRECTIONS Look at each set of terms below. On the line
provided, write the letter of the term that does not relate to the
others.

_____ 1. a. island hopping   _____ 3. a. Battle of Midway

        b. Battle of Coral Sea   b. Douglas MacArthur

        c. Battle of Leyte Gulf   c. Bataan Death March

        d. heavy casualties on land   d. the Philippines

_____ 2. a. Chester Nimitz   _____ 4. a. Battle of Midway

        b. U.S. Pacific fleet   b. Bataan Death March

        c. Douglas MacArthur   c. Battle of Leyte Gulf

        d. kamikaze   d. aircraft carriers

DIRECTIONS Read each sentence and fill in the blank with the
word in the word pair that best completes the sentence.

_____ 5. Douglas MacArthur

_____ 6. Bataan Death March

_____ 7. Battle of Coral Sea

_____ 8. Battle of Midway

_____ 9. island hopping

_____ 10. kamikaze

a. battle between American and Japanese aircraft carriers that stopped invasion of Australia

b. strategy of attacking only key Pacific islands

c. the cause of thousands of deaths when the Japanese forced American and Filipino troops to walk to prison camps

d. the Japanese tactic of crashing planes into enemy ships

e. lost but eventually retook the Philippines

f. battle between the Allies and the Japanese navy in which the Allies badly weakened the Japanese navy

World War II

MAIN IDEAS
1. The Allies gained victory in Europe with Germany's surrender.
2. Nazis murdered millions of Jews and other people in the Holocaust.
3. Victory in the Pacific came after the United States dropped atomic bombs on Japan.

Key Terms and People

Battle of the Bulge key battle at the Ardennes forest; Allies were victorious after an initially successful German attack

Harry S. Truman vice-president who became president when Roosevelt died in 1945

Holocaust Nazi program of mass murder against the Jewish people

genocide extermination of an entire group of people

Manhattan Project secret American research program to develop the atomic bomb

atomic bomb weapon that produces tremendous power by splitting atoms

Lesson Summary

GERMANY SURRENDERS

After the D-Day invasion, hundreds of thousands of Allied troops landed in France. By August 1944 Allied troops had taken control of Paris from the Germans. At the same time, Soviet troops were headed for Germany from the east.

In December Hitler ordered a massive attack against the Allies, whose planes were grounded due to bad weather. Germany pushed forward about 65 miles, creating a bulge in the front lines. The Allies recovered quickly and their planes were able to fly. The Allied victory at the **Battle of the Bulge** put Germans on the defensive for the rest of the war.

The Allies began bombing raids on German cities. These raids killed thousands of civilians. As Allied troops surrounded Berlin, Hitler

> How did the Allied airplanes' initial inability to fly affect the Battle of the Bulge?
>
> _____
> _____
> _____

committed suicide. The Germans surrendered on
May 8, 1945.

Roosevelt died before the German surrender.
Harry S. Truman became president and faced the
challenge of winning the war in the Pacific.

Underline the name of the U.S. president who accepted the German surrender.

HORRORS OF THE HOLOCAUST

As the Allied forces liberated Europe, they
discovered that stories of the **Holocaust** were
true. Soon after taking power, Hitler had begun a
campaign against the Jews. The Nazis destroyed
or seized property and moved the Jews to ghettos
and concentration camps.

Hitler's "final solution" was **genocide**. He
planned to get rid of all of the Jewish people,
killing millions in death camps. About 6 million
Jews were killed during the Holocaust. The Nazis
also murdered millions of other people.

What was Hitler's "final solution"?

VICTORY IN THE PACIFIC

The Allied planners projected that an invasion of
Japan could cause more than 1 million Allied
deaths. They had another option, based on
research results of the **Manhattan Project**. When
Japanese leaders refused to surrender, President
Truman gave the order to use the **atomic bomb**.

On August 6, 1945, an atomic bomb was
dropped above the Japanese city of Hiroshima.
Almost 80,000 people were killed instantly.
Thousands died later. Japanese leaders refused to
surrender, and a second bomb was dropped on
the city of Nagasaki. The Japanese surrendered
on September 2, 1945.

Underline the name of the two cities where atomic bombs have been dropped during a war.

AFTER THE WAR

After six years World War II was over. About 50
million people had been killed. More than half
of them were civilians. Economies were badly
damaged, and millions of people were left
without food, water, or shelter. Because the

Why did the United States have to take charge of much of the rebuilding in Europe and Asia?

United States was the strongest remaining power
in the world, it took on much of the job of
rebuilding.

CHALLENGE ACTIVITY

Critical Thinking: Make Judgments Was using
atomic bombs against Japanese cities the right
decision? Write a paragraph supporting your view.

DIRECTIONS Read each sentence and fill in the blank with the
word in the word pair that best completes the sentence.

1. Hitler's plan to eliminate the Jewish population was
   _____. (the atomic bomb/genocide)

2. The _____ was a temporary victory for the German army
   but ended in defeat. (Battle of the Bulge/Holocaust)

3. The secret American program to produce a super-weapon was known as the
   _____. (Holocaust/Manhattan Project)

4. The murder of millions of Jews in Europe by the Nazis is known as the
   _____. (Manhattan Project/Holocaust)

DIRECTIONS On the line provided before each statement, write **T** if
a statement is true and **F** if a statement is false. If the statement is
false, write the correct term on the line after each sentence that
makes the sentence a true statement.

_____ 5. About 6 million of Europe's Jewish population were victims of Hitler's
         planned genocide.

         _____

_____ 6. An atomic bomb that was dropped above Hiroshima killed almost
         80,000 people instantly.

         _____

_____ 7. The Manhattan Project ended Germany's ability to fight offensive
         battles.

         _____

_____ 8. Germany's "final solution" resulted in the Holocaust.

         _____

MAIN IDEAS
1. As World War II ended, leaders began planning the future of the postwar world.
2. The United States and the Soviet Union went from being allies to enemies after World War II.
3. Americans adjusted to postwar life.

Key Terms and People

Yalta Conference meeting of leaders to agree on postwar strategies

Nuremberg trials postwar trial of Nazi leaders for war crimes

United Nations organization dedicated to resolving international conflicts

superpowers powerful countries who influenced events in their parts of the world

Cold War struggle for global power between the United States and the Soviet Union

containment policy of preventing the Soviet Union from expanding its influence

Truman Doctrine policy of providing aid to help countries fight communism

Marshall Plan U.S. grants and loans to fund European recovery from World War II

North Atlantic Treaty Organization mutual defense alliance of United States, Canada, Iceland, and nine Western European nations

GI Bill of Rights bill offering veterans aid for education, housing, and businesses

Fair Deal domestic programs and civil rights protections proposed by Truman

Lesson Summary
THE FUTURE OF THE POSTWAR WORLD

At the **Yalta Conference**, Allied leaders strongly supported an international peacekeeping group. They also agreed that nations set free from Germany should be able to create their own governments. After the war, Germany was divided into four parts. The United States, Soviet Union, Great Britain, and France each controlled

> Why do you think Germany was divided into four sections?
>
> _____
>
> _____

Guided Reading Workbook

Lesson 1, *continued*

one part. Inside the Soviet section, Berlin was also divided.

Allied leaders formed a court to try Nazi leaders. At the **Nuremberg trials**, 19 Nazis were convicted of crimes against humanity. In separate trials, Japan's wartime leader as well as seven other Japanese leaders were convicted and sentenced to death.

In 1944 world leaders met to plan the **United Nations (UN)**. The goal of the UN was to settle global conflicts peacefully. One of the first major actions of the UN was the division of Palestine into separate Arab and Jewish states. Israel joined the United Nations in 1949.

> What was the purpose of the United Nations?
>
> _____
>
> _____

FROM ALLIES TO ENEMIES

After the war, conflicts arose between the United States and the Soviet Union. Both were former allies and **superpowers**. Stalin expanded control over the nations of Eastern Europe. This helped lead to the **Cold War**.

The United States had new policies based on **containment** of the Soviet Union. These policies included the **Truman Doctrine**. This provided aid to countries to help fight communism. The **Marshall Plan** was created to help make war-ravaged Europe stable. The **North Atlantic Treaty Organization (NATO)** member countries promised to defend each other if attacked. The Soviet Union created the Warsaw Pact. This rival alliance unified military command between the Soviet Union and its satellite countries in Europe.

> Underline the word that describes the postwar policy of the United States toward Soviet expansion.

POSTWAR AMERICA

As veterans returned from war, new laws and the **GI Bill of Rights** eased their transition. Rationing ended and prices went up. Unions demanded pay raises and went on strike. The president and Congress took action to gain more control over labor disputes.

> What caused Truman to lose some of his support in the South?
>
> _____
>
> _____
>
> _____

Guided Reading Workbook

Many African American soldiers came back to find prejudice and bigotry. President Truman supported their demands for civil rights laws. Although that support caused him to lose political strength in the South, he won reelection in 1948. He campaigned on the promise of a **Fair Deal**.

CHALLENGE ACTIVITY

Critical Thinking: Make Judgments Should Axis leaders have been held responsible for actions ordered by their governments? Why or why not?

DIRECTIONS Look at each set of terms below. On the line provided, write the letter of the term that does not relate to the others.

_____ 1. a. containment
   b. Cold War
   c. North Atlantic Treaty Organization
   d. Fair Deal

_____ 2. a. Yalta Conference
   b. GI Bill of Rights
   c. Fair Deal
   d. civil rights

_____ 3. a. United Nations
   b. Truman Doctrine
   c. North Atlantic Treaty Organization
   d. Nuremberg trials

_____ 4. a. Nuremberg trials
   b. Truman Doctrine
   c. containment
   d. Marshall Plan

DIRECTIONS Match the terms in the first column with their correct definitions from the second column by placing the letter of the correct definition in the space provided before each term.

_____ 5. United Nations

_____ 6. containment

_____ 7. Truman Doctrine

_____ 8. GI Bill of Rights

_____ 9. Marshall Plan

_____10. North Atlantic Treaty Organization

a. mutual defense alliance of the U.S., Canada, Iceland, and nine Western European nations

b. the U.S. policy of preventing the Soviet Union from expanding its influence

c. U.S. grants and loans given to help European recovery after World War II

d. policy stating that the U.S. government would give aid to foreign countries to fight communism

e. bill that offered veterans money for education and loans for homes

f. established by world leaders to settle international conflicts peacefully

The Cold War

Lesson 2

MAIN IDEAS
1. The United States fought Communist North Korea in the Korean War.
2. Fear of Communists led to a new Red Scare at home.
3. President Eisenhower faced Cold War crises around the world.

Key Terms and People

Mao Zedong Communist leader who established the People's Republic of China

38th parallel line that marked the division between North Korea and South Korea

Joseph McCarthy Wisconsin senator who made charges of communism in the government and the military

hydrogen bomb nuclear weapon far more powerful than the atomic bomb

arms race rush by the United States and the Soviet Union to build more weapons

Sputnik world's first artificial satellite, launched by the Soviet Union in 1957

brinkmanship willingness to go to the brink of war to stop communism

Lesson Summary
THE KOREAN WAR
The Cold War quickly spread from Europe to Asia. The Communists in China, led by **Mao Zedong**, gained control of the country. Many Americans worried that all of Asia might soon become Communist.

The Allies had divided Korea at the **38th parallel**. The Soviet Union controlled the northern half. The United States controlled the southern half. In 1950 North Korean troops invaded South Korea. The UN sent troops from the United States and 15 other countries to help South Korea. General Douglas MacArthur was given command of these forces. After his troops captured the North Korean capital, hundreds of thousands of Chinese soldiers joined North Korea.

> **Why did UN troops go to Korea in 1950?**
> _____
> _____
> _____

In 1951 the two sides reached a stalemate on the 38th parallel. Dwight D. Eisenhower was elected president in 1952. He promised to end the war. A truce in 1953 finally stopped the war. Once again, Korea was divided.

> **What do you think "a stalemate on the 38th parallel" means?**
> _____
> _____
> _____

A NEW RED SCARE

The first Red Scare came after the Russian Revolution in 1917. After World War II, people in the United States again began to fear that Communists would take over. Starting in 1947 Congress held hearings to look into Communist influence in the movie industry. Spy cases also increased concerns. Wisconsin senator **Joseph McCarthy** charged that Communists were inside the government and even in the U.S. Army. He had no concrete proof, so he made up some of the charges. He ruined many people's careers. The Senate later condemned his actions.

> **Why do you think Americans were afraid of communism?**
> _____
> _____
> _____

EISENHOWER AND THE COLD WAR

Cold War tension rose around the world. The development of the **hydrogen bomb** led to a nuclear **arms race** between the United States and the Soviet Union. When *Sputnik* was launched in 1957, the United States rushed to launch its own satellite. NASA was a new agency charged with carrying out space research.

Eisenhower did not agree with Truman's policy of containment. Instead, he wanted to turn back the Communist gains. Eisenhower supported the plan of **brinkmanship**. He used the Central Intelligence Agency (CIA) to protect democracy in places such as Iran and Guatemala.

In 1956 Egypt threatened to nationalize the Suez Canal. The United States and the Soviet Union worked together to prevent war. But the Cold War would continue despite this mutual aid.

> **Underline the name of the first artificial Earth satellite.**

> **Why would the United States and the Soviet Union work together when Egypt seized the Suez Canal?**
> _____
> _____

CHALLENGE ACTIVITY

Critical Thinking: Analyze Write a paragraph about the similarities and differences of brinkmanship and containment.

DIRECTIONS Read each sentence and fill in the blank with the word in the word pair that best completes the sentence.

1. The Soviet Union beat the United States to space when it launched _____ into orbit. (a hydrogen bomb/*Sputnik*)

2. _____ ruined many careers by accusing people in the U.S. government of being Communists. (Joseph McCarthy/Mao Zedong)

3. After World War II, Korea was divided by the _____. (arms race/38th parallel)

4. _____ was the result of the United States and the Soviet Union building more and more weapons. (Brinkmanship/The arms race)

5. _____ was more powerful than the atomic bomb. (The hydrogen bomb/*Sputnik*)

DIRECTIONS Write two adjectives or descriptive phrases that describe the term, person, or event.

6. Mao Zedong _____

_____

7. Joseph McCarthy _____

_____

8. hydrogen bomb _____

_____

9. arms race _____

_____

10. *Sputnik* _____

_____

The Cold War

MAIN IDEAS
1. America's economy boomed in the 1950s.
2. Americans enjoyed new forms of popular culture.
3. Social critics found fault with 1950s society.

Key Terms and People

baby boom a significant increase in the number of babies born after World War II

Sun Belt southern and western states that offered a warm climate year-round and low tax rates

urban renewal a plan to improve services and housing in deteriorating cities

beats young writers, or "beatniks," who criticized society with unusual writing styles and rebellious behavior

Lesson Summary
AMERICA'S ECONOMY IN THE 1950S

After the war, the American economy grew rapidly. People had money to spend. They felt financially secure. Many young people married and started families. This led to a **baby boom**.

People moved to new parts of the country for better jobs and quality of life. Many businesses and workers moved to the **Sun Belt**. The population in this region doubled in 30 years. New highways linked the whole country.

Highways made it easier for people to live in the suburbs and still work in the city. New growth in the suburbs drew many new homebuyers. By 1970 more people lived in the suburbs than in cities.

Many families enjoyed the comfort and ease of suburban life. Others criticized it as being heavily based on consumer culture and encouraging conformity. Some suburbs would not sell homes to African American families.

> **Why did the baby boom start after the end of the war?**
> _____
> _____
> _____

> **Why did some people criticize life in the suburbs?**
> _____
> _____
> _____

As white middle-class families moved from the cities, tax income in the cities declined. As a result, city services were reduced. This hurt people who could not afford to leave the cities. The federal government began an **urban renewal** program to improve city life.

Why did cities need money from the federal government for urban renewal programs?
_____
_____
_____

AMERICAN POP CULTURE

American life changed quickly in the 1950s. People began shopping in malls and eating at new fast-food restaurants. By the end of the decade, 90 percent of households had a television set. That meant that people all over the country shared the same experiences of watching news, entertainment, and sports.

New styles of music developed in the 1950s. African American jazz musicians helped create a type of music known as Bebop. Bebop was a complex jazz style played at a very fast pace. At the same time, rock 'n' roll was sweeping the nation. Teenagers powered the rock 'n' roll revolution by buying most of the records sold in the late 1950s. Like jazz in an earlier era, many adults were concerned and they criticized the new forms of music.

Underline the name of two new music styles that developed in the 1950s.

SOCIAL CRITICS

Many people were not happy with the way American society was going. Women had few job choices. Writers found fault with greed and conformity. Beatniks, or **beats**, used unusual writing styles and rebellious behavior to pass judgment on society. Many young people related to the beats. They also identified with defiant characters in popular movies.

What did many young people find appealing about beats?
_____
_____

CHALLENGE ACTIVITY

Critical Thinking: Analyze Would you prefer to live in a city or a suburb? Write a paragraph explaining the reasons for your choice.

| baby boom | Sun Belt |
| beats | urban renewal |

DIRECTIONS Use the four words or phrases from the word list to
write a summary of what you learned in the lesson.

_____

_____

_____

_____

_____

_____

_____

DIRECTIONS On the line provided before each statement, write **T** if
a statement is true and **F** if a statement is false. If the statement is
false, write the correct term on the line after each sentence that
makes the sentence a true statement.

_____ 1. The <u>urban renewal</u> drew many businesses and workers to its warm
climate and low tax rates.

_____

_____ 2. The <u>baby boom</u> produced new literature that challenged the rules of
society.

_____

_____ 3. The government started <u>urban renewal</u> programs to help save cities
with problems.

_____

_____ 4. The <u>baby boom</u> was a population explosion after World War II.

_____

The Vietnam War Years

MAIN IDEAS
1. President Kennedy confronted Communist threats around the world.
2. The United States and the Soviet Union raced to send a person to the moon.
3. The Cold War conflict in Vietnam led the United States into war.

Key Terms and People

Peace Corps program that sent volunteers to developing countries to help with projects such as digging wells and building schools

Fidel Castro Cuban rebel leader who led a revolution and established a Communist government

Berlin Wall Cold War barrier of concrete and barbed wire that separated East and West Berlin in Germany into two parts

Cuban missile crisis attempt by the Soviet Union to send nuclear missiles to Cuba; U.S. Navy formed a blockade to prevent Soviet ships from bringing in weapons

Neil Armstrong American astronaut; the first man to walk on the moon

Edwin "Buzz" Aldrin crewmate of Neil Armstrong; second man to walk on the moon

Ho Chi Minh leader of Communist revolution against the French in Vietnam

domino theory concern that if one nation became Communist, nearby nations would follow

Vietcong guerrilla fighters opposed to the South Vietnamese government

Lesson Summary
KENNEDY CONFRONTS COMMUNISM

President Kennedy was devoted to stopping communism. He used military forces and nonmilitary programs, such as the **Peace Corps**. In 1959 **Fidel Castro** organized a Communist government in Cuba. The CIA began training Cuban exiles to invade the island. However, the invasion, which occurred at the Bay of Pigs, was a disaster.

The Soviet Union threatened to take over West Berlin in 1961. When the Soviets were unable to

> **What methods did President Kennedy use to stop the growth of communism?**
>
> _____
>
> _____
>
> _____

do so, the **Berlin Wall** was created. In 1962 the **Cuban missile crisis** lasted for 13 days and ended when the Soviet Union stopped placing nuclear weapons in Cuba. The crisis led to the Limited Nuclear Test Ban Treaty.

RACE TO THE MOON

One aspect of the Cold War during the 1960s was the space race. In 1961 the Soviet Union sent the first man, Yuri Gagarin, into space. Then, in 1961 Alan Shepard Jr. made the first American space flight. John Glenn orbited Earth in 1962. In 1969 **Neil Armstrong** and **Edwin "Buzz" Aldrin** became the first people to walk on the moon.

> Who were the first people to walk on the moon?
> _____
> _____

CONFLICT IN VIETNAM

One of the most serious and devastating events of the Cold War took place in Vietnam. After World War II, **Ho Chi Minh** led nationalists to take Vietnam from the French. He wanted to establish a Communist government. The United States supported the French with military aid because of the **domino theory**. The French surrendered in 1954, and Vietnam was divided into North Vietnam and South Vietnam.

> Underline the theory that caused the United States to be worried about Vietnam having a Communist government.

The United States hoped that Ngo Dinh Diem would win elections. He would then be able to unify Vietnam under a non-Communist government. When Diem canceled elections in South Vietnam, a civil war began. South Vietnamese troops fought the **Vietcong**, who were supplied by the North. The United States sent military supplies and advisers to South Vietnam. Diem began to lose popularity. In November 1963 military officers took power.

> What action started the civil war in Vietnam?
> _____
> _____

CHALLENGE ACTIVITY

Critical Thinking: Identify Cause and Effect Do you think that the United States would have sent

people to the moon in 1969 if there had not been
the Cold War? Write a paragraph explaining your
answer.

DIRECTIONS Look at each set of terms below. On the line
provided, write the letter of the term that does not relate to the
others.

_____ 1. a. Neil Armstrong
       b. Fidel Castro
       c. Alan Shepard Jr.
       d. Edwin "Buzz" Aldrin

_____ 2. a. Peace Corps
       b. Ho Chi Minh
       c. Fidel Castro
       d. Soviet Union

_____ 3. a. Cuban missile crisis
       b. Berlin Wall
       c. Bay of Pigs
       d. Neil Armstrong

_____ 4. a. Cuban missile crisis
       b. Ho Chi Minh
       c. Vietcong
       d. domino theory

DIRECTIONS Match the terms in the first column with their correct
definitions from the second column by placing the letter of the
correct definition in the space provided before each term.

_____ 5. Fidel Castro

_____ 6. Berlin Wall

_____ 7. Cuban missile crisis

_____ 8. Ho Chi Minh

_____ 9. domino theory

_____ 10. Vietcong

a. the idea that one Communist
    victory would lead to another

b. a period of 13 days when nuclear
    war seemed likely

c. led a Communist revolution in
    Cuba

d. an army of Communist guerrilla
    forces

e. built by the East German
    government

f. wanted to free Vietnamese people
    with a Communist revolution

The Vietnam War Years

MAIN IDEAS
1. President Johnson committed the United States to victory in Vietnam by expanding U.S. involvement.
2. American soldiers faced new challenges fighting the Vietnam War.
3. The Tet Offensive was an important turning point in the war.

Key Terms and People

Tonkin Gulf Resolution congressional resolution that gave military authority to President Johnson

Ho Chi Minh Trail paths and tunnels used as a supply route by the North Vietnamese

escalation policy of increased involvement in the war followed by President Johnson

William Westmoreland commander of the U.S. ground forces in Vietnam

search-and-destroy missions policy of finding hidden enemy camps and destroying them with massive firepower and air strikes

Tet Offensive series of coordinated surprise attacks launched by the Vietcong and North Vietnamese on the Vietnamese New Year (Tet)—January 30, 1968

doves opponents of the war

hawks supporters of the war

Lesson Summary
JOHNSON COMMITS TO VICTORY

President Johnson was determined to prevent Communists from taking over South Vietnam. After a naval battle in 1964, he asked Congress to give him the authority to take military action. Congress did this by passing the **Tonkin Gulf Resolution**.

The first U.S. combat troops were sent to Vietnam in March 1965. Along with the ground troops, air strikes were ordered to disrupt the **Ho Chi Minh Trail**. In addition to bombs, U.S. warplanes released chemicals. The chemicals burned forests and killed vegetation. By 1968 more than a million tons of explosives had been

> What was President Johnson's reason for becoming involved in the conflict in Vietnam?
>
> _____
>
> _____

> Circle the year in which combat troops from the United States were first sent to Vietnam.

dropped on Vietnam, and still, the Communists
waged war.

U.S. SOLDIERS IN VIETNAM

Starting in 1965 President Johnson followed a
policy of **escalation** in the war. By 1968 more
than 500,000 U.S. troops were in Vietnam.
American generals thought it would be a quick
victory.

There were few front lines in the Vietnam War.
General **William Westmoreland** developed a
strategy based on **search-and-destroy missions**.
The Vietcong and North Vietnamese answered
with guerrilla tactics, secret traps, and land mines.
They received supplies from China and the Soviet
Union. Many South Vietnamese civilians were
driven from their homes and U.S. troops lost
their support.

From what countries did
the North Vietnamese army
and the Vietcong receive
supplies?

_____

_____

More than 2 million Americans served in the
Vietnam War. About one-quarter were drafted.
Many came from minority groups and poor
families. The Americans won many battles;
however, they were rarely able to hold their gains.

Circle the number of
soldiers from the United
States who served in the
Vietnam War.

TURNING POINTS IN VIETNAM

By the end of 1967 military leaders declared
victory was near. On January 30, 1968, however,
the Vietcong and North Vietnamese launched the
Tet Offensive. The massive attack shocked
Americans. People started to question why the
United States was waging this long, involved war.

Television brought violent images of the war
into American homes. A bitter split developed
between **doves** and **hawks**. The doves believed the
war was diverting resources from more important
needs at home. The hawks wanted increased
spending since they wanted to win the war, which
was thought of as part of the Cold War. After
the My Lai massacre, even more Americans
questioned the war.

How could television
coverage of the war affect
public opinion about the
war?

_____

_____

_____

CHALLENGE ACTIVITY

Critical Thinking: Draw Inferences Why was the Vietnam War considered to be part of the Cold War, even though American forces were fighting the Vietnamese, not Soviet troops?

doves	Ho Chi Minh Trail	Tonkin Gulf Resolution
escalation	search-and-destroy missions	William Westmoreland
hawks	Tet Offensive	

DIRECTIONS Use the eight terms and names from the word bank to write a summary of what you learned in the lesson.

_____

_____

_____

_____

_____

_____

_____

_____

_____

_____

DIRECTIONS Write two adjectives or descriptive phrases that describe the term, person, or event.

1. Tonkin Gulf Resolution _____

_____

Lesson 2, continued

2. escalation _____

_____

3. Tet Offensive _____

_____

4. doves _____

_____

5. hawks _____

_____

> **MAIN IDEAS**
> 1. Opinions about the Vietnam War divided American society in the 1960s.
> 2. The war under Nixon expanded from Vietnam to Laos and Cambodia.
> 3. The Vietnam War ended in 1973, but it had lasting effects on Vietnam and the United States.

Key Terms and People

Students for a Democratic Society student group active in protesting the Vietnam War

hippies people who "dropped out" of mainstream society and built a counterculture during the 1960s that emphasized individual freedom, nonviolence, and communal sharing

Richard M. Nixon Republican president elected in 1968

Henry Kissinger national security adviser to President Nixon

Vietnamization strategy of having the South Vietnamese army take over the fighting

Twenty-Sixth Amendment constitutional amendment lowering the voting age to 18

War Powers Act law passed in 1973 that requires congressional approval to commit troops to an armed struggle for more than 60 days

Vietnam Veterans Memorial granite wall in Washington, DC, which lists the names of soldiers killed or missing in Vietnam; designed by Maya Ying Lin

Lesson Summary
SOCIETY IN THE 1960S

Many people began to criticize the war. College students, including the **Students for a Democratic Society**, criticized the draft. They also protested companies that made weapons. Antiwar demonstrations were held at almost 75 percent of all American college campuses. Many people felt the antiwar movement was a rejection of established values. **Hippies** wanted individual freedom, communal sharing, and nonviolence.

President Johnson lost a lot of public support because of the war. He chose not to seek

> **Where did a large number of antiwar protests take place?**
>
> _____

reelection in 1968. Republican nominee **Richard M. Nixon** promised to restore order and won the election.

THE WAR UNDER NIXON

President Nixon wanted U.S. troops removed from Vietnam, but he did not want to suffer an American defeat. Together with **Henry Kissinger**, he created the plan of **Vietnamization**. As he pulled U.S. troops out of Vietnam, Nixon approved bombing raids on Cambodia and Laos. He wanted to disrupt Vietcong supply lines.

George McGovern, the Democratic candidate in 1972, opposed the war. He hoped the passage of the **Twenty-Sixth Amendment** would help him attract new voters. Many older voters feared a McGovern win. This fear caused Nixon an easy victory.

> **Why did Nixon approve the bombing raids on Cambodia and Laos?**
> _____
> _____

THE VIETNAM WAR ENDS

American troops were removed permanently from Vietnam by 1974. When new fighting broke out, the United States refused to send troops back. The Communists took Saigon in 1975 and created the Socialist Republic of Vietnam.

The war was responsible for a loss of confidence in the U.S. government. The **War Powers Act** was passed in 1973, which restricted the power of the president to commit troops to war.

U.S. forces suffered heavy losses in Vietnam. Soldiers who returned from the war were not always treated as heroes. Many struggled to readjust to civilian life. America tried to heal by erecting the **Vietnam Veterans Memorial** in 1982.

> **In what year did Saigon fall to the Communists?**
> _____

> **What happened to soldiers who returned from Vietnam?**
> _____
> _____
> _____

CHALLENGE ACTIVITY

Critical Thinking: Analyze Why do you think
many of the protests against the Vietnam War
occurred on college campuses?

Henry Kissinger	Twenty-Sixth Amendment
Richard M. Nixon	Vietnam Veterans Memorial
Students for a Democratic Society	War Powers Act

DIRECTIONS Answer each question by writing a sentence that
contains a term or name from the word bank.

1. Who was President Nixon's national security adviser?

_____

_____

2. What law allowed 18-year-olds to vote?

_____

_____

3. What was one of the most active protest groups in 1968?

_____

_____

4. What monument was designed by Maya Ying Lin?

_____

_____

5. What presidential candidate promised to restore order to the United States?

_____

_____

6. What law made it more difficult for the president to send troops into battle?

_____

_____

The Civil Rights Movement

Lesson 1

> **MAIN IDEAS**
> 1. Civil rights leaders battled school segregation in court.
> 2. The Montgomery bus boycott helped end segregation on buses.
> 3. Students organized sit-ins to protest segregation.

Key Terms and People

Thurgood Marshall attorney and first African American Supreme Court justice

Brown v. Board of Education lawsuit challenging the segregation of public schools

Little Rock Nine first black students to attend a school forced to integrate in Little Rock, Arkansas

Emmett Till African American teen from Chicago, Illinois, who was murdered while visiting family in the South; the murder made people aware of southern racism

Rosa Parks African American woman who refused to give up her seat on a public bus to a white passenger

Montgomery bus boycott nonviolent protest of segregation on public transportation

Martin Luther King Jr. Baptist minister and civil rights leader who inspired nonviolent protests against discrimination

sit-in demonstration in which protesters sit down and refuse to leave

Student Nonviolent Coordinating Committee student activists who organized nonviolent civil rights protests and voter registration drives

Lesson Summary
BATTLING SEGREGATION

In 1896 the Supreme Court created the doctrine of "separate but equal." This meant segregation was allowed as long as facilities were equal. Many states, in both the North and South, had separate schools for black and white students. Usually the schools for white students received better funding.

The National Association for the Advancement of Colored People (NAACP)

> Why was the "separate-but-equal" doctrine ineffective in education?
>
> _____
>
> _____
>
> _____

Lesson 1, *continued*

worked to end public school segregation.
Thurgood Marshall argued in the ***Brown v. Board
of Education*** case. In 1954 the Supreme Court
ruled that public school segregation was illegal.
The following year, the court ordered the
integration of all public schools.

Only three southern school districts began to
integrate. Others chose to implement gradual
integration plans. When the **Little Rock Nine**
tried to enter a newly integrated school,
Arkansas's governor sent troops to stop them.
Eventually, President Eisenhower sent federal
troops to escort the students.

Although some advances were made against
segregation, blacks still faced racism in the
South. When **Emmett Till** of Chicago, Illinois,
was murdered while visiting relatives in
Mississippi, Americans began to understand the
need for action.

> Underline the name of the
> legal case that led to
> desegregation of public
> schools.

> Who made it possible for
> the Little Rock Nine to
> enter school?
> _____
> _____

MONTGOMERY BUS BOYCOTT

Public transportation services were still
segregated in the South. The NAACP chose
to fight against this on buses in Montgomery,
Alabama. When **Rosa Parks** chose not to give
up her bus seat to a white passenger, she was
arrested. A group of local black leaders
organized the **Montgomery bus boycott**. It was
led by **Martin Luther King Jr.** The boycott lasted
for 381 days. It sparked protests in other cities. In
1956 the Supreme Court ruled that segregation
on public transportation was illegal.

> Underline the name of the
> nonviolent protest in
> Montgomery, Alabama, led
> by Martin Luther King Jr.

SIT-INS AND THE SNCC

Many private businesses in the South were also
segregated. In 1960 four students in Greensboro,
North Carolina, chose to challenge this prejudice.
They held a **sit-in** at a lunch counter. Other black
students began similar nonviolent protests.

> What was the purpose of
> the sit-in at the lunch
> counter in Greensboro?
> _____
> _____

Guided Reading Workbook

Businesses were integrating, but slowly. The
Student Nonviolent Coordinating Committee
(SNCC) formed to keep up the fight for civil
rights. The SNCC organized many protests. The
organization also worked to register black voters.

CHALLENGE ACTIVITY
Critical Thinking: Explain Why did the federal
government need to intervene to protect the civil
rights of African Americans?

DIRECTIONS Match the terms in the first column with their correct
definition from the second column by placing the letter of the
correct definition in the space provided before each term.

_____ 1. Thurgood Marshall

_____ 2. *Brown* v. *Board*
            of Education

_____ 3. Emmett Till

_____ 4. Little Rock Nine

_____ 5. Rosa Parks

_____ 6. Montgomery bus boycott

_____ 7. Martin Luther King Jr.

_____ 8. sit-in

_____ 9. Student Nonviolent
            Coordinating Committee

a. a person who was arrested for
   refusing to give up a bus seat to a
   white passenger

b. an attorney for the NAACP who
   fought against segregation

c. a Baptist minister who became a
   civil rights leader

d. the group of African American
   students who integrated a white
   high school

e. a group formed to continue the
   fight for civil rights and organize
   protests

f. a protest by African Americans in
   Alabama over segregation on public
   transportation

g. a type of protest that took place at
   lunch counters in 1960

h. a case that led the Supreme Court
   to declare segregation illegal

i. a teen from Chicago whose murder
   made people more aware of racism
   in the South

DIRECTIONS Write two adjectives or descriptive phrases that describe each term.

10. *Brown* v. *Board of Education* _____

_____

11. Little Rock Nine _____

_____

The Civil Rights Movement

MAIN IDEAS
1. John F. Kennedy was elected president in 1960.
2. Civil rights leaders continued to fight for equality.
3. Lyndon B. Johnson became president when Kennedy was assassinated.
4. Changes occurred in the civil rights movement in the late 1960s.

Key Terms and People

John F. Kennedy U.S. president elected in 1960; youngest person elected president

Freedom Rides series of protests in which black and white passengers tried to integrate southern bus stations

Medgar Evers head of the NAACP in Mississippi who was murdered in 1963

March on Washington massive civil rights demonstration in 1963

Lyndon B. Johnson U.S. president after Kennedy was assassinated

Civil Rights Act of 1964 banned segregation and workplace discrimination

Voting Rights Act of 1965 law protecting African Americans' voting rights

Great Society Johnson's program to end poverty and racial injustice

Black Power movement that called for African American power and independence

Malcolm X leader who combined ideas about independence with teachings of Islam

Lesson Summary
KENNEDY ELECTED

While campaigning, **John F. Kennedy** supported civil rights, so many blacks voted for him. But as president, he acted slowly. He did not want to lose support in Congress for his New Frontier proposals, such as the space program and aid for the poor.

> Why was progress on civil rights slow during Kennedy's presidency?
>
> _____
>
> _____
>
> _____

THE FIGHT FOR RIGHTS CONTINUES

Bus stations had not yet been integrated. It continued even after the Supreme Court stated that it was illegal. Civil rights groups organized

Lesson 2, *continued*

protests including the **Freedom Rides**. After
attacks by white mobs, some groups stopped the
rides. However, other groups refused to give in.

In 1963 Martin Luther King Jr. led civil rights
marches in Alabama. He was arrested for
marching without a permit. Once he was set free,
he led new marches. Americans were shocked by
the brutal treatment of marchers and by the
murder of Mississippi's NAACP head **Medgar
Evers**. As support grew for civil rights legislation,
African American leaders held the **March on
Washington**.

What do you think was the purpose of the March on Washington?
_____
_____
_____

JOHNSON BECOMES PRESIDENT

Kennedy was assassinated in 1963. **Lyndon B.
Johnson** became president. He urged Congress to
pass civil rights laws. He later signed the **Civil
Rights Act of 1964**. Activists worked to register
southern African American voters. The **Voting
Rights Act of 1965** gave the federal government
new powers to secure voting rights.

Underline the names of the two civil rights laws passed during Johnson's administration.

President Johnson was reelected in 1964 by a
large margin. He saw this win as support for his
Great Society programs. These included
Medicare, Medicaid, and funding for housing
and education. Congress soon passed most of his
reforms.

CHANGES IN THE CIVIL RIGHTS MOVEMENT

Many young activists were angered by the slow
progress of the civil rights movement as a result
of nonviolent protests. **Black Power** movement
leaders, such as Stokely Carmichael, called for
African American power, independence, and
control of their own communities.

Malcolm X rejected integration as a goal of
civil rights. He and some others believed that
blacks had a right to defend themselves, with
violence if necessary. Frustration led to riots in
many cities. When Martin Luther King Jr. was

How did the Black Power movement differ from earlier civil rights movements?
_____
_____
_____

killed in 1968, more than 100 cities erupted into riots.

CHALLENGE ACTIVITY

Critical Thinking: Make Judgments Are nonviolent protests more effective than violent protests? Write a paragraph about your position.

DIRECTIONS Look at each set of terms below. On the line provided, write the letter of the term that does not relate to the others.

_____ 1. a. Lyndon B. Johnson
         b. Great Society
         c. Black Power
         d. Medicaid

_____ 2. a. Civil Rights Act of 1964
         b. March on Washington
         c. Great Society
         d. Voting Rights Act of 1965

_____ 3. a. Freedom Rides
         b. Black Power
         c. Stokely Carmichael
         d. Malcolm X

_____ 4. a. March on Washington
         b. Freedom Rides
         c. voter registration drives
         d. John F. Kennedy

DIRECTIONS Read each sentence and fill in the blank with the word in the word pair that best completes the sentence.

5. Malcolm X was a part of the _____ movement. (Great Society/Black Power)

6. White mobs viciously attacked protesters taking part in the _____. (March on Washington/Freedom Rides)

7. President Johnson tried to end poverty with a set of social programs called the _____. (Great Society/Civil Rights Act of 1964)

8. Segregation was banned in all public places by the _____. (Civil Rights Act of 1964/Voting Rights Act of 1965)

9. The _____ movement pushed for increased African American independence. (Freedom Rides/Black Power)

10. President _____ was more successful in passing civil rights reforms than his predecessor. (Lyndon B. Johnson/John F. Kennedy)

The Civil Rights Movement

MAIN IDEAS
1. Hispanic Americans organized for civil rights and economic opportunities.
2. The women's movement worked for equal rights.
3. Other Americans also fought for change.

Key Terms and People

Cesar Chavez Hispanic activist who founded the United Farm Workers

Dolores Huerta helped form the United Farm Workers and worked for fair wages

United Farm Workers union that fought for migrant farm workers' rights

Betty Friedan women's rights activist and founder of NOW

National Organization for Women organization to fight for opportunities for women

Shirley Chisholm first African American woman elected to the U.S. Congress

Equal Rights Amendment constitutional amendment to outlaw all discrimination based on gender

Phyllis Schlafly leader of opposition to Equal Rights Amendment

American Indian Movement group formed to fight for Native Americans' rights

Earl Warren Supreme Court Chief Justice who helped extend individual rights

Warren Court issued landmark decisions that further defined individual rights

Disabled in Action activist organization for rights of disabled people

Lesson Summary

HISPANIC AMERICANS ORGANIZE FOR CHANGE

The success of African Americans encouraged others to fight for their rights. **Cesar Chavez** and **Dolores Huerta** founded a union that was later known as the **United Farm Workers**. The union worked for better pay and humane working conditions for migrant farm workers.

Chavez inspired the Chicano movement. This struggle for political power for Hispanics had far-reaching consequences. For example, schools were required to provide teachers who could speak Spanish and other languages while

> **What was one consequence of the Chicano movement?**
>
> _____
> _____
> _____

students learned English. Also, the Voting Rights Act of 1975 made it possible for people to vote in languages other than English.

THE WOMEN'S MOVEMENT

Women had fewer job opportunities than men before the 1960s. The Equal Pay Act required employers to pay men and women the same salary for the same jobs.

Activists questioned women's roles in society, too. **Betty Friedan** helped found the **National Organization for Women** (NOW) in 1966. In 1968 **Shirley Chisholm** was the first African American woman elected to Congress. In the early 1970s many women supported the **Equal Rights Amendment** (ERA). **Phyllis Schlafly** led a conservative group opposed to the ERA. Congress approved it in 1972. However, it fell three states short of ratification.

> Why was the Equal Pay Act passed?
> _____
> _____
> _____

> Underline the phrase that indicates why the Equal Rights Amendment did not become part of the Constitution.

OTHER VOICES FOR CHANGE

Other groups called for an end to intolerance, too. The **American Indian Movement** (AIM) fought for Native Americans' rights. They wanted control over their own lands. Then Supreme Court Chief Justice **Earl Warren** and the **Warren Court** made many landmark decisions. They extended rights to groups that faced discrimination. Lastly, **Disabled in Action** (DIA) worked to change laws and make people aware of problems faced by disabled people. The Education of Handicapped Children Act and the Americans with Disabilities Act passed. They outlawed discrimination against disabled people.

> How did the Americans with Disabilities Act help people who are disabled?
> _____
> _____
> _____

CHALLENGE ACTIVITY

Critical Thinking: Identify Cause and Effect List three consequences of the changes that occurred during the civil rights era. What differences might you see today without these changes?

Betty Friedan	Disabled in Action	Phyllis Schlafly
Cesar Chavez	Earl Warren	Shirley Chisholm
Dolores Huerta	National Organization for Women	United Farm Workers

DIRECTIONS On the line provided before each statement, write **T** if a statement is true and **F** if a statement is false. If the statement is false, write the correct term on the line after each sentence that makes the sentence a true statement.

_____ 1. <u>Betty Friedan</u> was the first African American woman elected to Congress.

_____

_____ 2. <u>Phyllis Schlafly</u> helped defeat the Equal Rights Amendment.

_____

_____ 3. The <u>Equal Rights Amendment</u> attempted to improve working conditions and pay for migrant workers.

_____

_____ 4. The <u>American Indian Movement</u> created equal opportunities for women.

_____

_____ 5. <u>Dolores Huerta</u> worked for fair wages, benefits, and humane working conditions for Hispanic farm workers.

_____

_____ 6. <u>Cesar Chavez</u> worked to improve economic opportunities for Hispanic Americans.

_____

_____ 7. Efforts of the group <u>United Farm Workers</u> led to new laws such as the Rehabilitation Act of 1973.

_____

_____ 8. As Chief Justice of the Supreme Court, <u>Earl Warren</u> helped extend individual rights.

_____

Searching for Order

MAIN IDEAS
1. Americans faced domestic challenges, including an energy and economic crisis.
2. Nixon's foreign policy led to improved relations with Communist powers.
3. The Watergate scandal forced Nixon to resign.
4. Gerald Ford became president upon Nixon's resignation and faced many challenges.

Key Terms and People

stagflation stagnant economic growth and high inflation

Organization of Petroleum Exporting Countries (OPEC) group of oil-producing nations that controls the production and sale of oil

realpolitik foreign policy based on practical American interests, not on ideals

Strategic Arms Limitation Talks (SALT) agreements between the United States and the Soviet Union limiting nuclear weapons

détente period of less hostile relations between United States and Soviet Union

Watergate scandal involving the Nixon administration

Gerald Ford vice-president who became president when Nixon resigned in 1974

pardon order granting freedom from punishment

Lesson Summary
DOMESTIC CHALLENGES

President Nixon proposed major shifts in policy. His New Federalism limited the federal government's power. He promised to restore law and order and reduce welfare spending. His four Supreme Court appointments changed the court.

Nixon faced **stagflation**, partly due to rising oil prices. Prices rose due to decisions made by the **Organization of Petroleum Exporting Countries** (OPEC). OPEC cut off sales to the U.S. as a result of U.S. support for Israel.

> How could OPEC control the price of oil in the United States?
>
> _____
> _____

NIXON'S FOREIGN POLICY

Nixon adopted a new approach to foreign policy, based on **realpolitik**. Some choices, such as

Lesson 1, *continued*

backing harsh military governments that were friendly to the United States, were controversial. The approach also led to a change in Cold War politics. To widen the split between China and the Soviets, Nixon had meetings with China. Soviet leaders then became more open, leading to the **Strategic Arms Limitation Talks**. This was followed by a period of **détente** between the U.S. and the Soviet Union.

> **How did the strategy of realpolitik lead to a controversial foreign policy?**
> _____
> _____
> _____

THE WATERGATE SCANDAL

In 1972 the Democratic National Committee offices in the Watergate Hotel were broken into. Nixon denied involvement. He went on to win reelection easily. After the election, newspaper stories began to reveal a cover-up, calling it **Watergate**.

The Supreme Court ordered Nixon to turn over tapes of White House discussions to Congress. These tapes showed his involvement in the scandal. A congressional committee passed articles of impeachment, so Nixon resigned on August 8, 1974.

> **Underline the action taken by the congressional committee that led to Nixon's resignation.**

FORD AS PRESIDENT

After Nixon left office, his vice-president, **Gerald Ford**, became president. Ford granted Richard Nixon a **pardon**. Oil prices stayed high, and stagflation continued. The U.S. trade deficit increased. Ford created a plan to fight inflation, but it met resistance in Congress. Ford and Congress compromised, but inflation and unemployment remained high.

CHALLENGE ACTIVITY

Critical Thinking: Analyze Write a paragraph explaining how a policy of working with China could improve relations with both China and the Soviet Union.

détente	pardon	stagflation
Gerald Ford	realpolitik	Strategic Arms Limitation Talks
Organization of Petroleum Exporting Countries		Watergate

DIRECTIONS On the line provided before each statement, write **T** if
a statement is true and **F** if a statement is false. If the statement is
false, write the correct term or name from the word bank on the line
after each sentence that makes the sentence a true statement.

_____ 1. A period of <u>realpolitik</u> led to more open relations between the United
States and the Soviet Union.

_____

_____ 2. The combination of rising prices and high unemployment was called
<u>stagflation</u>.

_____

_____ 3. Richard Nixon avoided possible punishment because of his <u>Strategic
Arms Limitation Talks</u>.

_____

_____ 4. During the 1970s, oil production in the Middle East was controlled by
the <u>Strategic Arms Limitation Talks</u>.

_____

_____ 5. Nixon's presidency was brought down by <u>Watergate</u>.

_____

_____ 6. <u>Gerald Ford</u> became president when Richard Nixon resigned.

_____

Searching for Order

MAIN IDEAS
1. American society debated key social issues during the 1970s.
2. Jimmy Carter was elected president in 1976.
3. Carter had successes as well as failures in foreign policy during his administration.

Key Terms and People

affirmative action practice of giving special consideration to nonwhites or women to make up for past discrimination

Rachel Carson biologist and author of *Silent Spring*; helped start the environmental movement

Jimmy Carter former governor of Georgia; elected United States president in 1976

human rights basic rights and freedoms of all people

apartheid South African system of racial segregation

sanctions economic penalties

Camp David Accords a peace agreement that resulted from meetings between Jimmy Carter and the leaders of Israel and Egypt

Iran hostage crisis holding of approximately 52 U.S. embassy personnel for more than a year in Iran

Lesson Summary
SOCIAL ISSUES OF THE 1970S

In the 1970s immigration patterns into the United States began to change. Most of the new immigrants came from Latin America and Asia. The average age of the population increased as birth rates decreased. These changes raised the question of how to balance the views of all Americans.

Although the Equal Rights Amendment did not become law, the women's movement made gains. Laws such as Title IX improved opportunities for women in education and college sports. **Affirmative action** programs helped many women and nonwhites. Opponents of the

> Why did some people oppose affirmative action programs?
>
> _____
>
> _____

programs felt that all gender- and race-based preferences were unfair.

The environment also became a major issue in the 1970s. *Silent Spring* by **Rachel Carson** inspired a national movement to improve the environment. Congress passed laws to limit the release of pollutants. The Environmental Protection Agency was formed to put these laws into effect.

CARTER ELECTED

In 1976 Democrats selected **Jimmy Carter** to run against Ford in the presidential election. Carter won because he was a Washington "outsider." Events in the government had caused people to lose trust.

Carter had serious tests once elected. The nation faced high unemployment and inflation. Carter also wanted to lessen dependence on imported oil. Even though Democrats controlled Congress, he was not able to pass his national energy plan. His goal to expand nuclear power was stopped after an accident occurred at the Three Mile Island power plant.

> **Why would being a Washington "outsider" help Jimmy Carter get elected?**
> _____
> _____
> _____

CARTER AND FOREIGN POLICY

Carter rejected the policy of realpolitik. Instead he promoted **human rights**. To push reform and an end to **apartheid**, he called for **sanctions** against South Africa. Détente broke down when Carter criticized the Soviets for human rights abuses. Then the Soviet Union invaded Afghanistan, and Carter ended arms control talks. He also did not let U.S. athletes take part in the 1980 Olympics in Moscow.

President Carter worked to ease tensions in the Middle East. The peace treaty known as the **Camp David Accords** is one of his greatest triumphs. However, many Americans lost their

> **Circle the name of the country in which apartheid was practiced.**

> **How did the Iran hostage crisis affect the presidency of Jimmy Carter?**
> _____
> _____

trust in Carter's leadership during the **Iran hostage crisis**.

CHALLENGE ACTIVITY

Critical Thinking: Make Judgments Was a boycott of the 1980 Olympics in Moscow an appropriate response to the Soviet invasion of Afghanistan? Why or why not?

DIRECTIONS Read each sentence and fill in the blank with the word in the word pair that best completes the sentence.

1. Democrats hoped that _____, a Washington "outsider," could defeat Gerald Ford in the presidential election. (Rachel Carson/Jimmy Carter)

2. The _____ hurt the public's faith in Carter's presidency. (Iran hostage crisis/Camp David Accords)

3. The practice of _____ improved the number of opportunities for African Americans. (affirmative action/apartheid)

4. The economic penalties imposed by one country on another are called _____. (human rights/sanctions)

5. President Carter brought the leaders of Israel and Egypt together to sign _____. (sanctions/the Camp David Accords)

6. While Nixon based his foreign policy on realpolitik, Carter based foreign policy on _____. (apartheid/human rights)

7. _____ drew attention to environmental issues when the book *Silent Spring* was published. (Rachel Carson/Jimmy Carter)

8. President Carter opposed South Africa's policy of segregation called _____. (sanctions/apartheid)

DIRECTIONS Look at each set of terms below. On the line provided, write the letter of the term that does not relate to the others.

_____ 9. a. Jimmy Carter
       b. human rights
       c. affirmative action
       d. sanctions

_____ 10. a. Camp David Accords
       b. apartheid
       c. Middle East
       d. Jimmy Carter

Searching for Order

MAIN IDEAS
1. President Reagan based his policies on conservative ideas.
2. Reagan took a tough stand against communism in his foreign policy.

Key Terms and People

Ronald Reagan United States president elected in 1980

supply-side economics economic theory based on increasing investment by making sharp tax cuts

deficit amount by which a government's spending exceeds its income

Iran-Contra affair controversial plan for the United States to sell missiles to Iran and give the profits to Nicaraguan rebels known as Contras

Mikhail Gorbachev Soviet leader who initiated changes in government policies and new freedoms for Soviet people

Lesson Summary
REAGAN AND CONSERVATIVE IDEAS

Ronald Reagan defeated Jimmy Carter in the 1980 election by asking voters, "Are you better off than you were four years ago?" His goal was to cut taxes and reduce regulations on businesses. These were conservative ideas.

Reagan's economic policies were based on **supply-side economics**. Many Democrats opposed his policies. However, Congress agreed to tax cuts. They backed cuts in spending for social programs such as school lunches and food stamps. A short recession occurred, but the economy improved in 1983. Spending on defense grew faster than tax revenues. This resulted in a growing **deficit**.

One of Reagan's goals was to reduce government control of key industries. He believed that this would help improve the economy. Congress agreed and reduced many laws governing major industries.

> **What question did Ronald Reagan ask voters during the 1980 election?**
>
> _____
>
> _____

Reagan appointed three Supreme Court justices in office. The implications of this were that the court changed. It became more conservative. One nominee, Sandra Day O'Connor, became the first woman to serve on the Supreme Court in 1981. Reagan ran for reelection in 1984. At the time the economy was booming, and he was reelected by a landslide.

REAGAN AND FOREIGN POLICY

President Reagan was against communism and the Soviets. He supported anti-Communist governments in Central America and gave them aid. Critics of this policy said that the aid helped military governments that violated human rights in their own homelands.

The U.S. administration helped the anti-Communist rebels, called Contras, in Nicaragua. This led to fear that the U.S. could be drawn into a war. Congress passed a law banning U.S. military aid to the Contras. The **Iran-Contra affair** became a national controversy in 1986 because it violated the congressional ban. However, Congress found no evidence of illegal actions by Reagan.

During his first term, Reagan stopped arms talks with the Soviet Union and expanded the U.S. military. Attempts by the Soviet Union to match U.S. spending on arms hurt its economy. **Mikhail Gorbachev** started political and economic reforms. He established new freedoms. Reagan and Gorbachev signed a treaty eliminating medium-range nuclear weapons.

> Circle the name of the anti-Communist rebel group in Nicaragua.

> Why didn't the Iran-Contra affair affect Ronald Reagan the same way that Watergate affected Richard Nixon?
> _____
> _____
> _____

CHALLENGE ACTIVITY

Critical Thinking: Analyze Were ending negotiations and building up the military effective ways to deal with the Soviet Union?

| deficit | Mikhail Gorbachev | supply-side economics |
| Iran-Contra affair | Ronald Reagan | |

DIRECTIONS Use the five terms and names from the word bank to write a summary of what you learned in the lesson.

_____

_____

_____

_____

_____

_____

DIRECTIONS Match the terms in the first column with their correct definitions from the second column by placing the letter of the correct definition in the space provided before each term.

_____ 1. Ronald Reagan

_____ 2. supply-side economics

_____ 3. deficit

_____ 4. Iran-Contra affair

_____ 5. Mikhail Gorbachev

a. the result of massive defense spending and lower taxes

b. illegal dealings by Reagan's government

c. believed in cutting taxes and the size of government

d. reformed the Soviet economy

e. the theory that if people and businesses paid less taxes, they would invest more in the economy

Searching for Order

MAIN IDEAS
1. Major global changes took place during the presidency of George H. W. Bush.
2. During Bill Clinton's presidency, the nation experienced scandal, economic growth, and the rise of terrorist threats.

Key Terms and People

George H. W. Bush United States president elected in 1988

Saddam Hussein Iraqi dictator

Operation Desert Storm U.S.-led multinational coalition offensive to drive Iraqi troops from Kuwait

Colin Powell former chairman of the joint chiefs of staff and highest ranking African American to serve in the U.S. military; later served as secretary of state

Bill Clinton Arkansas governor who became United States president in 1992

North American Free Trade Agreement (NAFTA) treaty to end trade barriers between the United States, Canada, and Mexico

Madeleine Albright first woman to become secretary of state; appointed by Bill Clinton

terrorism use of violence by individuals or small groups to advance political goals

Lesson Summary
GEORGE H. W. BUSH

Ronald Reagan had been a very popular president. This helped his vice-president, **George H. W. Bush**, win the 1988 election.

Reforms in the Soviet Union and in other Communist governments continued. In October 1989 East Germans overthrew their Communist government. The Berlin Wall was torn down. Several Soviet Republics declared independence. The Soviet Union soon fell apart.

President Bush called for all countries to work together. The idea was tested when **Saddam Hussein** invaded Kuwait in 1990 and refused to

> How did reforms in the Soviet Union affect Eastern Europe?
> _____
> _____
> _____

withdraw. That year a U.S.-led multinational coalition formed to drive Iraqi forces from Kuwait. **Operation Desert Storm** was led by American generals Norman Schwarzkopf and **Colin Powell** and lasted about six weeks.

CLINTON'S PRESIDENCY

Most Americans supported Bush's handling of the Gulf War. Nevertheless, the struggling economy was the most important issue of the 1992 election. **Bill Clinton** told the American people that he would focus on improving the economy. He won the 1992 election in a three-way race.

Clinton's budget focused on reducing the deficit by cutting spending and raising taxes. He convinced Congress to support the **North American Free Trade Agreement**.

> **What was the goal of Clinton's budget? How did he plan to achieve that goal?**
> _____
> _____

In 1994 Republicans gained control of both houses of Congress. They promised lower taxes and smaller government. Clinton won reelection in 1996 with the help of a strong economy. Clinton's second term was dominated by questions about his personal conduct. Investigators charged that he had had an improper relationship with a White House intern and lied about it under oath. In 1998 the House of Representatives voted to impeach Clinton on charges of obstruction of justice. The Senate acquitted him of those charges in 1999.

> **Why was President Clinton impeached?**
> _____

Clinton named **Madeleine Albright** as the first female secretary of state. She helped the United States adjust to its new role of being the world's only remaining superpower. U.S. troops played a peacekeeping role in disputes in the Balkan region.

> **Circle the name of the first woman appointed to the position of secretary of state.**

In the 1990s **terrorism** became a major issue. Terrorist attacks occurred in Oklahoma City and in other places around the world.

CHALLENGE ACTIVITY

Critical Thinking: Make Inferences Why might
President George H. W. Bush have wanted to
form a coalition of other nations before
launching Operation Desert Storm?

DIRECTIONS Read each sentence and fill in the blank with the
word in the word pair that best completes the sentence.

1. Trade barriers between the United States, Canada, and Mexico disappeared
   because of the _____.
   (North American Free Trade Agreement/Operation Desert Storm)

2. _____ is the use of violence to advance one's political
   goals. (Operation Desert Storm/Terrorism)

3. _____ led the United States during Operation Desert
   Storm. (George H. W. Bush/Bill Clinton)

4. Bill Clinton's secretary of state was _____. (Madeleine
   Albright/Colin Powell)

5. The United Nations launched an offensive called _____
   to remove Saddam Hussein from Kuwait. (terrorism/Operation Desert
   Storm)

6. _____ is the highest-ranking African American ever to
   serve in the U.S. military. (Colin Powell/Madeleine Albright)

7. _____ was the leader of Iraq who invaded Kuwait in
   1990. (Colin Powell/Saddam Hussein)

DIRECTIONS On the line provided before each statement, write **T** if
a statement is true and **F** if a statement is false. If the statement is
false, write the correct term on the line after each sentence that
makes the sentence a true statement.

_____ 1. <u>George H. W. Bush</u> was governor of Arkansas before becoming president.

_____

_____ 2. <u>Bill Clinton</u> was president of the U.S. when the Soviet Union broke up.

_____

_____ 3. <u>Colin Powell</u> helped Bill Clinton handle disputes in the Balkan region.

_____

The Twenty-First Century

Lesson 1

MAIN IDEAS
1. George W. Bush won the disputed 2000 presidential election.
2. Americans debated the future of the War on Terror that began after terrorists attacked the United States.
3. The American economy and job market rapidly changed and affected domestic policy.

Key Terms and People

Al Gore Bill Clinton's vice-president; Democratic presidential nominee in 2000

George W. Bush U.S. president elected in 2000

World Trade Center important business center in New York City

Pentagon headquarters of the U.S. Department of Defense, near Washington, DC

al-Qaeda fundamentalist Islamic terrorist group

Osama bin Laden wealthy Saudi exile who led al-Qaeda

weapons of mass destruction weapons capable of killing thousands of people

service economy most jobs are providing services rather than producing goods

globalization growing connections between economies and cultures worldwide

Lesson Summary
THE 2000 PRESIDENTIAL ELECTION

The 2000 election was a race between Democrat **Al Gore**, Bill Clinton's vice-president, and Republican **George W. Bush**, son of the former president and governor of Texas.

The votes were too close on election night to declare either candidate a winner. In Florida, a recount was needed. The winner in Florida would win the election. Gore supporters asked for a manual recount in several counties. The Supreme Court ruled against the manual recount. Bush was declared the winner. He became the first president in more than 100 years to win the electoral vote but not the popular vote. Congress soon passed the $1.35 trillion tax-cut plan Bush had promised.

> **Why was the vote count in Florida so important in the 2000 election?**
>
> _____
> _____
> _____

FIGHTING TERRORISM

On September 11, 2001, two airplanes crashed into the **World Trade Center** in New York City. Another plane crashed into the **Pentagon**. A fourth plane crashed in rural Pennsylvania. Terrorists had hijacked all these planes. The hijackers were part of a terrorist group called **al-Qaeda**, led by **Osama bin Laden**. Thousands of people were killed. President Bush vowed to punish those responsible.

In October 2001 the United States attacked Afghanistan, where al-Qaeda was based. U.S. troops drove Afghanistan's leaders, the Taliban, from power. However, bin Laden could not be located until many years later.

President Bush and other world leaders thought that Iraqi leader Saddam Hussein posed a threat. They believed that he had not given up Iraq's **weapons of mass destruction**. Some countries wanted to keep looking for weapons. However, a coalition of allies led by the United States and Britain attacked Iraq. Saddam's government had been toppled. Yet, the war dragged on.

THE NEW GLOBAL ECONOMY

The country has moved toward a **service economy**. Also, **globalization** has changed how companies do business. It also has changed how countries interact.

A financial crisis began in 2007 when the housing market collapsed. The United States had entered an economic depression. The government passed legislation to try to help the country's economy. These stimulus efforts added jobs, increased GDP, and lowered unemployment. The country's economy began to recover over time.

> What type of attacks did al-Qaeda terrorists use on September 11, 2001?

> Circle the name of the country in which American officials expected to find Osama bin Laden.

> How did the United States government help rebuild the country's economy?

CHALLENGE ACTIVITY

Critical Thinking: Make Judgments Do you think
the decision to attack Iraq was justified? Why or
why not?

Al Gore	globalization	service economy
al-Qaeda	Osama bin Laden	weapons of mass destruction
George W. Bush	Pentagon	World Trade Center

DIRECTIONS Use at least seven terms or names from the word
bank to write a summary of what you learned in the lesson.

_____

_____

_____

_____

_____

_____

_____

_____

DIRECTIONS Write two adjectives or descriptive phrases that
describe the term or person.

1. Al Gore _____

_____

2. World Trade Center _____

_____

3. al-Qaeda _____

_____

4. Osama bin Laden _____

_____

5. globalization _____

_____

The Twenty-First Century

Lesson 2

MAIN IDEAS
1. The nation faced difficult challenges during President Bush's second term.
2. Barack Obama became the first African American president of the United States.
3. The Obama administration worked toward economic recovery and ending the Iraq War.
4. Donald J. Trump won the 2016 presidential election.

Key Terms and People

Department of Homeland Security cabinet department that protects American citizens from terrorism

USA PATRIOT Act law giving the government powers to protect against terrorism

Condoleezza Rice secretary of state during George W. Bush's second term

Nancy Pelosi first female Speaker of the House of Representatives

Barack Obama elected president of the United States in 2008 and reelected in 2012; first African American to serve as president

Patient Protection and Affordable Care Act law requiring that health care be available for all Americans

Lesson Summary
GEORGE W. BUSH

After 9/11 President George W. Bush created the **Department of Homeland Security** to help protect the United States from terrorism. Also, Congress passed the **USA PATRIOT Act** to protect citizens from possible terrorists. Some people have said that this law is unconstitutional. Some Americans also opposed U.S. fighting in the war in Iraq.

President Bush made important appointments to his cabinet and the Supreme Court. For example, **Condoleezza Rice** became the first female African American secretary of state.

The Democrats gained control of both houses of Congress in 2006. Democrat **Nancy Pelosi** became the first woman to be elected Speaker of the House of Representatives.

> Underline the words that describe the main goal of the Department of Homeland Security.

> What was one reason why the appointment of Condoleezza Rice was significant?
> _____
> _____
> _____

The way the Bush administration handled natural disasters, the Iraq War, and the economy brought much criticism. An economic recession in 2008 caused more problems. Many Americans became increasingly unhappy with the Bush administration.

BARACK OBAMA

Promising change, **Barack Obama** won the 2008 presidential election. In doing so, he became the nation's first African American president. Obama began his presidency by taking steps to help improve the economy.

President Obama then turned his attention to health care reform. He signed the **Patient Protection and Affordable Care Act**. Many people questioned whether the government should require that citizens have health care.

The Obama administration also focused on fighting terrorism. It pulled combat troops from Iraq. However, it increased military operations in Afghanistan. U.S. Special Forces located and killed Osama bin Laden. Later, the Obama administration began efforts to try to lessen the threat of ISIS, a growing terrorist group.

> **What changes did President Obama introduce?**
>
> _____
> _____
> _____

Gun violence proved to be a growing problem in the twenty-first century. Americans tried to end gun violence in schools and elsewhere. Yet citizens have differing opinions about gun use. In 2010 the Supreme Court held that local and state bans on handguns were unconstitutional. In 2013 President Obama proposed stricter federal gun-control laws.

> **What was President Obama's response to the Supreme Court's ruling about local and state bans on handguns?**
>
> _____
> _____

THE 2016 PRESIDENTIAL ELECTION

Republican Donald J. Trump won the 2016 presidential election. His opponent Democrat Hillary Clinton won the popular vote. However, Trump won 306 electoral votes. Only 270 electoral votes are needed to become President.

> **How many electoral votes did Trump win?**
>
> _____
> _____

CHALLENGE ACTIVITY

Critical Thinking: Make Judgments Find out more about the USA PATRIOT Act. Write a paragraph that tells whether you believe that the law is fair or unfair.

Barack Obama	Nancy Pelosi
Condoleezza Rice	Patient Protection and Affordable Care Act
Department of Homeland Security	USA PATRIOT Act

DIRECTIONS Answer each question by writing a sentence that contains at least one term or name from the word bank.

1. What cabinet group deals with terrorism in the United States?

_____

_____

2. What law gives the United States government many tools to fight terrorism?

_____

_____

3. Who became the first African American woman to hold the office of secretary of state?

_____

_____

4. Who was the first female to be elected Speaker of the House of Representatives?

_____

_____

5. What law required Americans citizens to have health insurance?

_____

_____

The Twenty-First Century

MAIN IDEAS
1. Technological advances continue to solve everyday problems.
2. The American population is aging and becoming more diverse than ever before.

Key Terms and People

Internet global system of computer networks

Information Revolution changes that made it easier and faster for people to access and share information

AIDS acquired immunodeficiency syndrome; disease that causes the body's immune system to shut down

ozone layer gas in the upper atmosphere that blocks harmful rays from the sun

global warming increase in Earth's temperature; also referred to as climate change

Medicare health care program that pays medical expenses for senior citizens

Social Security government program that pays benefits to retired Americans

Lesson Summary

TECHNOLOGY MOVES FORWARD

Technological changes and inventions have had a large effect on American life. Recently, use of the **Internet** has exploded. This has made it easier for people to share information. This **Information Revolution** helped fuel the economic boom of the 1990s. Tablets, cell phones, and laptop computers are just some of the current technology in use today.

Circle three types of technology in use today.

One problem people face because of technological innovations is cyberbullying. This kind of harassment happens online. It is done using text messages, email, or other electronic communication.

Despite this drawback, modern technology has many benefits. For example, technology is helping to facilitate medical research. The Human Genome Project was completed in 2003.

What effect has technology had on science and the environment? _____ _____

Researchers have made connections between genetics and disease. Researchers are also looking for new treatments for **AIDS**, which has killed more than 39 million people worldwide.

Scientists are looking for new ways to protect the environment. Banning the use of certain chemicals has reduced damage to the **ozone layer**. A 2004 report showed that the ozone layer is perhaps slowly being repaired. Concerns about **global warming** have led to the development of new kinds of transportation. These new vehicles use batteries, less gas, or fuels such as hydrogen, which produce less pollution.

Other scientists look beyond Earth to explore space. Today, human exploration of space continues on the International Space Station.

> Underline the sentence that describes one approach to solving the problem of global warming.

THE CHANGING AMERICAN POPULATION

The American population continues to grow and change. In 2005 about 14 percent of the country's total population was Hispanic. African Americans made up about 13 percent. Asian Americans were about 5 percent. In 2008 Barack Obama became the first African American to be elected president of the United States.

Immigration is a main cause of increased diversity in the United States. Certain push factors such as natural disasters or war lead people to leave their homelands. Pull factors such as the chance for a job attract immigrants to the United States.

The population of the United States is changing in another way. Americans are older than ever before. They depend more and more on programs that provide elder care. The costs of programs such as **Medicare** and **Social Security** are skyrocketing.

> How does the age of Americans affect the country's economy?
>
> _____
> _____
> _____

CHALLENGE ACTIVITY

Critical Thinking: Explain Write two paragraphs
that explain how your local community is
affected both by technology and changes in
population.

DIRECTIONS Match the terms in the first column with their correct
definitions from the second column by placing the letter of the
correct definition in the space provided before each term.

_____ 1. Internet

_____ 2. Information
          Revolution

_____ 3. AIDS

_____ 4. ozone layer

_____ 5. global warming

_____ 6. Medicare

_____ 7. Social Security

a. a layer of the atmosphere that protects
   people from harmful solar rays

b. program that pays retirement benefits to
   older citizens

c. program that pays health care costs of
   senior citizens

d. an often fatal medical condition affecting
   the body's immune system

e. a global system of computer networks that
   enables worldwide sharing of information

f. shaped the economy of the 1990s by
   changing how people and businesses
   communicated

g. changes in the climate that are most likely
   worsened by human air pollution

DIRECTIONS Read each sentence and fill in the blank with the
word in the word pair that best completes the sentence.

8. Senior citizens in the United States who need health care rely on
   _____. (Social Security/Medicare)

9. More than 23 million people have died of _____. (global
   warming/AIDS)

10. Banning the use of certain chemicals has reduced damage to the
    _____. (ozone layer/Internet)

11. Today, individuals share information electronically with others around the
    world through use of the _____. (Internet/Information
    Revolution)